1 25?

"Dear Charlie" Letters

"Dear Charlie" Letters

RECORDING THE EVERYDAY LIFE
OF A YOUNG 1854 GOLD MINER . . .
AS SET FORTH BY

Your Friend, Horace Snow

WITH SUITABLE GOLD RUSH ENGRAVINGS

Designed By Muriel Neavin

A Publication Of The
Mariposa County Historical Society

Published By:
Mariposa Museum and History Center, Inc.
P.O. Box 606
Mariposa, California 95338

Pioneer Publishing Company
Fresno, California 93704

Library of Congress Catalog Card Number 79-84190
ISBN 0-914330-22-5

Illustrated by engravings from:
  Hutchings' *California Magazine*, 1856-1862
  Beyond the Mississippi by Albert D. Richardson, 1867
  A La California by Colonel Albert S. Evans, 1874

Contents

Preface

Horace C. Snow, the writer of the "Dear Charlie" letters, was one of many young men who came to California to make their fortune in the gold fields. He, as an educated man, had the ability to see and a flair for expressing what he saw.

It was Muriel Neavin, artist, designer, historian, and a resident of Mariposa County since 1948, who generously agreed to prepare the exhibits for the Mariposa County Historical Society Museum. Muriel designed the exhibits for the first museum, located in the Masonic Building, where the "Dear Charlie" letters were a popular feature.

Since the opening of the new History Center on May 23, 1971, thousands of visitors have been enthusiastically lavish in their praise of the exhibits and, in addition, have been intrigued with the letters as a theme. Many visitors have expressed a desire to obtain a copy of these letters. Prompted by these frequent requests, Charles I. Wright, then president of the Society, appointed a Publication Committee, with Muriel Neavin as Editor. The letters merit our attention as a rich source of information on how a young miner and his partners lived their California gold-mining days in Mariposa County.

William Kimes

Introduction:
Dear Charlie Letters

On September 5, 1853, Horace C. Snow, a young man of good sense and good humor, said farewell to his home town of Bridgewater, Massachusetts. He put himself and his valise on board a ship in New York Harbor and sailed away to make his fortune in the gold fields of California. He traveled by side-wheeler steamer to Chagres, Panama, crossed the seventy-five mile Isthmus by dugout canoe and by mule, caught a ship at Panama City, and arrived in San Francisco on October 12, 1853.

With very little money in his pockets, he explored the gold camps, working at odd jobs to pay his way. Once his curiosity was satisfied, he walked to Mariposa County, southernmost mining district of the Mother Lode. There he joined his brother Hiram at Agua Frio. Hiram, at fifteen, had responded to the first gold stories of 1849 by sailing around the "Horn," a six to twelve month endurance test that not all '49ers survived. The story of Hiram's journey and his adventures as one of the earliest Agua Frio Creek miners would have made fascinating reading, but as Horace explained, "My brother fails to write home." Horace, however, was a dedicated correspondent who worked off his homesickness by writing to his friends. Apparently only Charles (Dear Charlie) E. Fitz behaved as a really "true chum" should, faithfully sending news from home. Stay-at-home Charlie, who was fascinated by descriptions of the Miner's Life, saved his friend's letters. These epistles (a favorite Snow word) were later passed on to members of the Horace Snow family and the Frees family, who generously presented them to the Mariposa County Historical Society.

When Horace Snow arrived in Agua Frio, he was just one more Yankee dropped into the California melting pot. By 1854 the original Spanish-Mexican population had become thoroughly diluted. Americans earning wages of five to ten dollars a month were tantalized by stories of thousand-dollar strikes and earnings of a hundred dollars a day. The word "gold" was a magnet to South Americans, Chinese, Australians, and to the Europeans fleeing their world of war and revolution. To Horace and other miners, California was almost a foreign land. Because of this feeling of strangeness and the knowledge that friends and family were at least four difficult weeks away, the "back home" states were referred to nostalgically as "America."

Forty-niners from "America" brought their Anglo-Saxon system of self-government to mining camps and the "Dear Charlie" letters record the rough-and-ready Americanization of a state that had been under Mexican rule only a few years before. Horace Snow's letters describe Mariposa County judges and juries, saloon brawls, gunfights, outlaws, and murders . . . as well as the everyday lives of hopeful gold seekers.

The towns of Agua Frio and Mariposa were sprawled beside their gold-filled streams on land that had watched over ancient Miwok Indian dwellings, then miners' tents, and finally the saloons, stables and false-front stores of a typical Sierra foothill camptown. A February 3, 1854 issue of the *Mariposa Chronicle* advertised an amazing choice of services and goods. Amazing, because most of the necessities and niceties were shipped via the 17,000-mile Cape Horn route. Horace chose to live frugally, saving his hard-won gold dust for the future, but if he had cared to behave in a "flashy" manner, he could have decorated his cabin with French wallpaper, tasseled draperies and Venetian carpets; he could have indulged in fancy clothes, exotic fruits from the Sandwich Islands (Hawaii), even a marble-topped billiard table; a dentist, a doctor, and a patent medicine druggist were ready to soothe away his ailments.

Horace Snow's adventure lasted twenty-one months. His "Dear Charlie" letters give today's readers an intimate view of a bright young man who chose to leave the safety of home, to try his luck in a faraway place, to work hard, to learn and to survive. His letters reveal his thoughts, beliefs and opinions; and poignantly, the rise and fall of his hopes.

A Lost Letter Found

Horace Snow's letters to Charlie brought California and the treasure hunters to life, but a very important episode was missing—his five weeks of travel between New York and San Francisco, from September 5 to October 12, 1853.

Now, thanks to a fragile, water-damaged, almost unreadable, wonderful letter donated to the Mariposa County History Center by grandson Huestis Snow and members of the Snow family, the "Dear Charlie Letters" can properly begin with Horace's first adventures, starting with the "Georgia Disaster." Although he describes the fear and panic and the helplessness of people trapped on a sinking ship, he does so in his own humorous style. However, the solemn accounts in various newspapers made it quite clear that the disintegration of a ship on the high seas was no laughing matter.

The California bonanza was a golden opportunity, not only for thousands of hopeful Argonauts, but also for ship owners who viewed the hordes of impatient men as their own personal gold mines. An armada of old vessels, dried-up antiques and sodden relics were resurrected from their resting places. Splintered timbers and rotten hulls were caulked and painted; the infirmities were concealed, but to sail on such an old fraud was a dreadful gamble. Even strong, seaworthy ships were destroyed by gales, fogs, and rocky shores. Horace had the bad luck to leave New York harbor on board a seagoing coffin called the "Georgia." She was a rough-riding ship and must have been especially torturous for friend Horace and the other steerage passengers.

E. S. Capron's book, *History of California*, published in

1854, described steerage as a "terrible place . . . men, women and children huddled together . . . in the very bottom of the vessel; a damp, dark, poorly-ventilated hole." And he observed, "the Georgia . . . is inferior."

Nevertheless, Horace survived his steerage accommodations, as well as his shipwreck, and once safely ashore, his luck seems to have improved. He escaped the dangers, horrors, and misfortunes suffered by so many Panama travelers; thieving porters, deadly fevers, and equally deadly bandits apparently passed him by. To Horace, traversing the Isthmus was a lark. He even made connections with the San Francisco-bound steamship *Oregon* without the usual long wait in dirty, steaming Panama City.

As he says in his letter, "The remainder of our voyage was very pleasant."

Horace Snow
California Bound

Sonora, November 27th, 1853

Dear Little Fitz

How a few dimes spent in the right way will separate us: no mistake Charlie, I am in California. The whole world and the rest of mankind couldn't make me believe last spring that I should be here now, especially when we were drawing near the Pacific Coast. What then was imagination has now become a reality.

Yes, I have seen the extreme point of Cape St. Lucas and the bold Sierra Nevada; have seen the Sacramento and the San Joaquin, been in South America and among the West Indies Islands and last of all sailed the two largest bodies of water in the world. My passage on the Atlantic side was very unpleasant. You probably have heard and read the particulars of the

---

The Disaster to the Steamship Georgia

Baltimore, Tuesday, Sept. 13
The Portsmouth *Globe* contains the purser's statement of the recent accident to the steamship *Georgia*. The vessel was much damaged, her hurricane deck, state-rooms, bulk-heads, &c., being cut up for firewood, all her wood having been washed away. Many of the passengers lost all their baggage and money. The gale did not abate till 2 a.m. on Thursday, when the British brig *Lady Chapman* came alongside, and remained with the *Georgia* till she reached Cape Henry.

But for the exertions of the passengers the vessel must have foundered. She was still leaking at the latest dates at the rate of six inches per hour.

—from *The New York Daily Times*

"Georgia Disaster." Therefore, I will not attempt a description. I suppose we encountered about as hard a storm as ever visits our coasts. Charlie, just imagine yourself three hundred miles from land, sick in your berth, weak, not having eaten anything for two days. The wind blowing a superlative hurricane—such as you can't conceive of on land—the waves running mountain high, dashing against the vessel—causing a report like thunder. The vessel sometimes immerses in water and then to have the cry come resounding down the hatchway—"All hands on deck and pump ship for she is sinking" and added to this cries and groans and screaming of passengers and you will have some idea of the position I was in. Well, after sometime I made out to get on deck—this was about ten o'clock in the evening, and never shall I forget the moments that I stood there with both hands hold of the railing for it was utterly impossible to stand without holding on with all of your might. The officers gave up the ship and the passengers of course thought it must be so. I tell you what Charlie, mathematics was of no account then. Physical force was all that saved us. Men were pulled out of their berths, dragged on deck and forced to work. I labored incessantly two days and three nights. I didn't look much like a Bridgewater student when I arrived at Norfolk, I tell you, and in fact I wasn't, was I? I never had a cap on the whole time and my old white coat looked as though it descended from "76."

The Georgia

Baltimore, Wednesday, Sept. 14
The passengers of the *Georgia*, having adopted resolutions that that vessel was unseaworthy and leaky when she left New York, Capt. Budd emphatically denies the charge.

The Norfolk papers state that the steamship *Georgia* would leave today for New York, though still leaking badly. Capt. Budd thinks she can be taken on with safety.

—from the *New York Daily Times*

I saw a great many things during the storm that caused me to laugh and quite hearty when the next moment we expected would be our last. Once I went to go through the second cabin and the ship gave a lurch and threw me down and I never had such a time in getting up in my life as then. I rolled and pitched and tumbled, first I would make up against one side of the room and then turn two or three somersets and strike my shoulders against the other side. You can conceive of my, and of all of our situations, by trying to stand on a perpendicular floor changing every moment.

Yes, I can also say that I have been in Virginia. We stayed there three days and were later taken off by the *Crescent City* and the remainder of our voyage was very pleasant. They have

---

Departure of the Crescent City from Norfolk with the Georgia's Passengers

Norfolk, Wednesday, Sept. 14 The steamship *Crescent City* sailed from this port yesterday afternoon with the *Georgia's* passengers for Aspinwall.
On her way here from New York, the *Crescent City* reports seeing two barks with loss of masts, both working to the northward.
—from the *New York Daily Times*, September 16, 1853

---

25 miles of railroad on the Isthmus which seemed much like home. Perhaps you would like to know the "modus operandi" of passing the Isthmus. Well, we land at Aspinwall, named after a merchant of N. York—take the cars 25 miles to Barbacoa. Here we take boat and go up the Chagres River 14 miles to Cruces. At Cruces, we take mules to Panama from 21 to 27 miles—or walk just as we would like. I chose to walk as did many others. Eighteen of us started in the morning and only one of them was able to keep up with me. I arrived in Panama at three o'clock, ahead of every mule but five, and two hours before any of the eighteen came in. So three cheers for Snow. Spear rode and I beat him over two hours. Ah! Another thing I

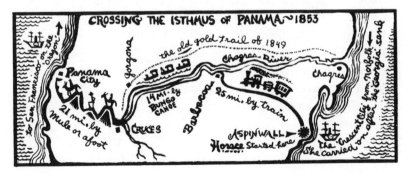

RAILWAY FARE—$8.00; CANOE AND CREW—$2.00; MULE HIRE—$8.00.

have crossed those mighty Andes. They commence away down about 50° don't they Charlie? "I should think you ought to know. You graduated first," says Charlie. Never mind, the first shall be last and the last first.

Crossing these mountains on the Isthmus is something like going on to Mt. Washington. I mean the road is about the same, the height is not so great. We found Yankees all the way through but not "Pilgrim Yankees" for they all kept liquors for sale. We often hear it said that you can trace your way across the desert by the bones of dead animals, but on the Isthmus you would do it by empty bottles. The sides of the road were literally covered with them. Panama once was a walled city, but now it is going to decay. To see how foolish these people were once, they laid out millions of money to wall the city in and left a small hill a little back commanding the town—perfectly defenseless—thinking if they were caged in they were perfectly safe. So Bolivar, with a few hundred men, drew up some canons and boomed away into them with perfect ease. The consequence was the total demolition of the whole inside, and they were forced to surrender.

The streets are paved and paved well, but two thirds of them are covered with grass. Everything is going to decay. Here we see the effects of Catholicism. I visited the cathedral at Panama and was more forcibly reminded of a puppet show than a church. There were all manner of images round on the walls—such as little children buy at toy shops—to pray to. I told Spear I would like to have a bushel of potatoes and if I wouldn't make a hussling among the graven images, it wouldn't of been because I didn't have a chance.

Everything was very dear on the Isthmus. Six cents for a cracker. $1.00 to sleep on the soft side of a pine board. The Sabbaths are not regarded any more than any other day. We were in Panama on the Sabbath and the city was choosing their officers. The stores were all open and a bullfight advertised for the afternoon.

Now we go along to the Land of Gold. We embarked on board the steamer *Oregon*, touched at Acapulco, Monterey and landed in San Francisco, the 17th day from Panama and 37th from New York. On going up from Panama we were only out of sight of land two days and this was when we were passing the Gulf of Tehuantapec. The land forms an iron bound coast all the way. Desolate and abrupt!

Well, Charlie, now we are in Cal. and by the way didn't we see oceans of whales on the Pacific side. What monstrous beings inhabit the briny deep. A fishing tackle for cod would hardly show in a whale.

Now as we are both in San Francisco, I think I'll stop, this being a good period, and talk about other things during the remainder of our chat. Therefore, next time I will commence at San Francisco.

Particulars of the Loss of the Steamship Georgia

October 13, 1853

The *Georgia* sailed from New York on the 5th . . . Shortly after getting to sea she encountered a gale . . . and sprung a leak . . . the passengers were bailing out the water with buckets. The nearest port, Norfolk, Va., was reached with difficulty on the 9th. The leak extinguished the fires before the vessel could get into shoal water . . . she went down in 20 feet of water.

A dispatch telegraphed to New York sent the *Crescent City* to Norfolk on the 11th. The *Georgia* is the second steamer of Law's line that has been lost within a month. The loss is not to be much regretted, unless by those whose pockets suffer. She was about the slowest steamer on the route, and should have been condemned . . . long since.

—from the *Daily Alta California*

The *Sacramento Daily Union* carried the same story on October 13, 1853, along with the passenger list of the *Oregon*. Surprisingly, the list of first and second class passengers included twenty-one women and at least twenty-nine children, as well as forty-some men. There were 250 steerage passengers, but their names were not listed. The name H. Snow was absent and since Horace left home with a nearly flat wallet, it seems that he must have traveled "steerage."

The fare from New York to California: first class, $100; second class, $75; third class (steerage), $50.

However, I am in Sonora at work at my trade. Shall go to mining in a few days. Have bought a claim and either expect to take out some or not to, one or the other. The rainy season has commenced. 'Tis pouring down most lustily, much to the gratification of thousands of miners. Charlie, how would you like to go mineralizing and dig out a piece of quartz rock with an ounce of gold on one end of it! Would it be a pretty specimen? I have seen lots of them. Some miners dug out a piece but a few rods from where I work that weighed 75 ounces of pure gold. Mentally, at $17.00 per ounce what as it worth? Divided 6 ways what would each man receive? Isn't this the country! 'Tis for some and many not.

Well, how does Bridgewater sagaciate? How much I have mourned to think I couldn't of stopped one or two days when on my way to this country. Not that it would have been very pleasant, but I could of had some good talks and a few that would of done me so much good. I look back now to those days when you and I roomed together as the happiest I ever enjoyed. I knew not than what the anguish of disappointment was!

How we used to study on our speeches!! And what able productions some of them were! How did you prosper with your paper? The Normal Offering edited and published. Didn't it tame Stephens?

Your class have probably passed another examination by now and entered on your last course. I suppose you are looked up to by the enterers as a model to pattern, your advice is sought and opinion respected! What a responsibility there rests upon your shoulders! Do you correspond with Mary Young? How I could like to see those "curious eyes" and hear her laugh again. How many a frolic you and I have had with her. She was a little afraid of me and in fact, who wouldn't be! Where is Phoebe Greene? Ah, she was the girl for me. I can see that good honest creature now, cheeks so red. How she would blush! Well there, what is the use to talk about these things. Obviously, an aggravation and still is! How is Potter? How much in advance of the class are they? Especially Burgess? Will he graduate with honors? Potter had such congeniality but lacked confidence and perserverance. Many a good time did we have over some of Stephen's pranks. Stephen had many curious notions but still I love him and why shouldn't I . . . both a victim of misplaced confidence. How did Nat enjoy life this fall? I should of thought he would of been in a prickly place around the school. But Nat has got plenty of brass. What did they say about me after I left? I wasn't conscious of passing events 'till I got to Fall Rivers. I would have given money, time and talent—especially the latter—to of had a good long talk with Jennie Fisher. She was one of my favorites but I hope she didn't suspect it. Next time you see or write to her you tell her to preserve my trumpet—for I shall be after it sometime.

Where is Frank?? I ought to write to her. Do you? If so give my regards and tell her I shall soon. Also Jennie Fisher. What a lot of questions I have asked you! Ten thousand more keep rushing into my mind all the time but *these* well answered—which you'll do, won't you?—will be enough to feed my intellect for a long time. How I would like to see you and have a good long talk. I could tell you some funny things! A person in coming to Cal. comes across much that a terra firma life time wouldn't originate. I must close but reluctantly. It seems as though I was with you. I almost thought I had on the *paper cap*. Now give me a good long answer. Don't stop inside of 8 pages. Your class mate—at the model—and friend,

Horace C. Snow

Mr. Charles H. Fitz

A Postscript Concerning the Georgia

Only five months after Horace Snow's narrow escape, the *Georgia* put out to sea and became a disaster again.

The Steamer Georgia
The Ship, Owners and
Commander Denounced

This steamer put into Norfolk on Friday night . . . a gale . . . carried away her entire forecastle and stove her boats.

Scenes on Board
(Some comments by passengers)

"It is a matter of astonishment that the *Georgia* ever reached a port." "The public will be indignant on hearing . . . that people were sent to sea on a rotten vessel." "I have had in my hand pieces of the vessel that crumbled with the pressure of my fingers."

Mr. E. E. Shain writes: "We went on the 6th . . . everything was pleasant enough except the horrible rocking of the 'old tub' . . . the sea was thrown into a tremendous excitement; two-thirds of those on board were down with sea-sickness . . . the sea carried away some 30′ of our bow . . . the greatest confusion prevailed; women praying, children screaming; some were shouting, and some were cursing George Law and some the ship."

"The pumps were all at work and gangs were bailing." They had to "shove in pillows and mattresses between the timbers . . . and nail canvas over . . . them."

—The *New York Daily Times* February 14, 1854

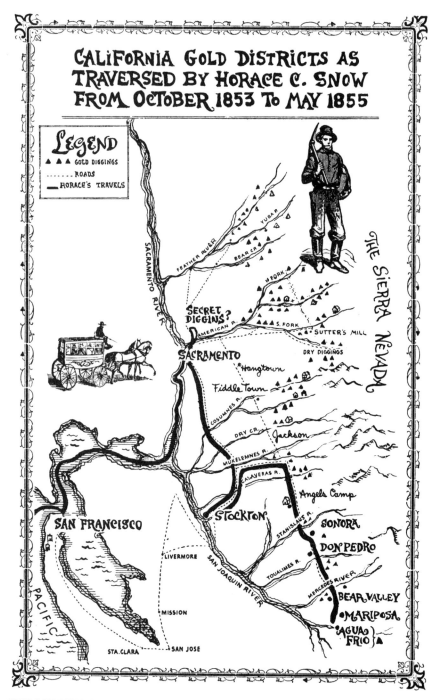

CALIFORNIA GOLD DISTRICTS AS TRAVERSED BY HORACE C. SNOW FROM OCTOBER 1853 TO MAY 1855

LEGEND
▲ ▲ ▲ GOLD DIGGINGS
.... ROADS
━━ HORACE'S TRAVELS

HORACE SNOW'S TRAVELS RECONSTRUCTED FROM DESCRIPTIONS IN HIS LETTERS AND FROM A MAP OF THE GOLD FIELDS PUBLISHED IN 1849 BY THE NEW YORK COMMERCIAL ADVERTISER.

LETTER 1

Horace Snow In 'Gold Rush' Country

Agua Frio, April 1st, 1854

Dear Charlie:

Your letter of January 18th arrived at its proper destination in two months and seven days, coming to hand March 25th.

Where it has been and what it has been doing, of course, it gave no account but judging from the looks I supposed it had been "prospecting." But like good Madeira, it was all the better from being old. The evening that I received your letter it happened to be my turn to prepare the supper, but I just seated myself in the most comfortable part of the cabin and told the boys that I should visit America for a short time and they must supply their insufficiency as best suited them. Charlie, do you know what it is to be pleased? Doubtlessly you have experienced something that passed for pleasure but the real genuine gratification of the conversative faculties no man in a civilized world ever enjoyed. That is according to Snow's reckoning. I have read your letter over three times and it will bear reading as many more. I had almost given up the idea of receiving a note from you and began to feel a little corner ways, but now I take it all back, or transfer it to Uncle Sam. Your letter itself was worth Mariposa County.

I was pleased to hear of your good success at school and also your confidence in keeping pace with the remainder of the Hon. 39th. If you don't leave them a long way in the distance, I fear you will climb but a short way toward the top of that noted

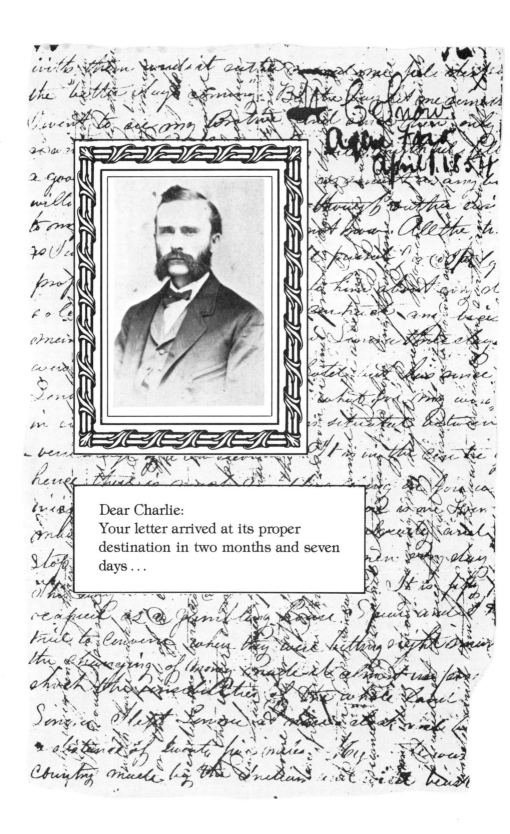

Dear Charlie:
Your letter arrived at its proper
destination in two months and seven
days . . .

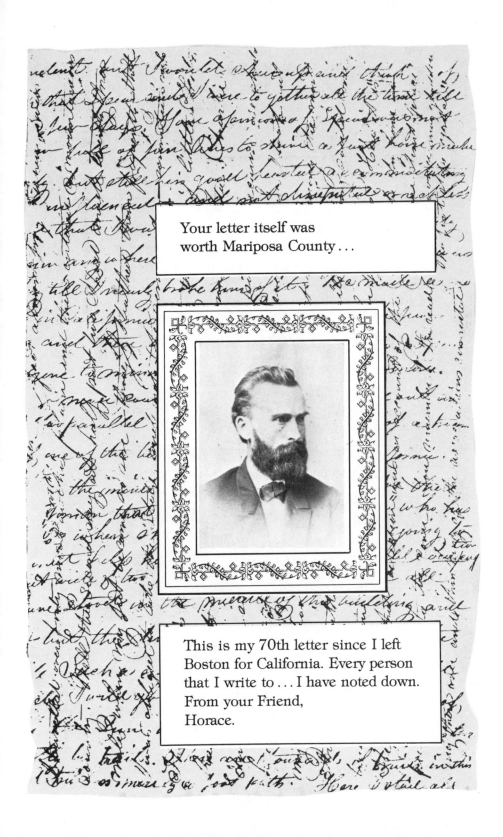

Your letter itself was
worth Mariposa County...

This is my 70th letter since I left
Boston for California. Every person
that I write to ... I have noted down.
From your Friend,
Horace.

elevation. If the class in which we had entered had been at par, I never should have been in California now. There wasn't that unity of feeling or disposition to press onward and obtain the cooperation of the teachers that characterized other classes.

April 2nd. This is a beautiful morning, Charlie. I rise this morning at half-past five and went down to the brook that runs by our cabin and had a fine bath. The water and atmosphere were very warm. I couldn't but help thinking of Bridgewater times when we used to go down and fathom the depths of that muddy stream. Nature looks splendid here today. The grass is about four inches high, thickly spotted with flowers of all colours, the trees and shrubs are preparing to leaf, the rays of the sun are warm and genial, the fragrance of the atmosphere is beautiful and refreshing and in fact, all vegetation is smiling. The birds sing, the frogs peep, the coyotes bark, the wolves howl, and the deer grazes at pleasure, all within sight of our cabin.

NATURE LOOKS SPLENDID HERE TODAY.

Before I give you a description of our mansion and location, I will go back to San Francisco where my last epistle closed in substance. I only remained in Frisco seven hours. During this time I visited the principle part of the city and saw the many wonders. There are many fine buildings in the city but the majority of them look like sugar boxes stacked up end ways.

I REMAINED IN FRISCO SEVEN HOURS.

Among the fine buildings is Adams & Co.'s, and what is more interesting, it is granite and was first built, finished and raised in China by Chinese workmen and then taken down and shipped to California and re-erected by the artisans. I visited the famous El Dorado Gambling House, where thousands have lost their last dollar and left in despair. Among the noted persons who sat behind a bank was a woman! There was no one betting at her table but by the looks of the money upon it some poor fellow had left much wiser and less "ore." What is meant by a bank is that some person will hire a room and spread a large quantity of money upon a table and open some kind of a game where anybody and everybody can come up and bet with them. I have seen thirty-five hundred silver dollars upon the table besides many thousands in gold.

Well, at four o'clock I took the steamer Senator and rode one hundred and sixty miles, as they call it, up the Sacramento River to the City of Sacramento. We arrived at Sac. about three o'clock in the morning. It was very dark going up the river, therefore I saw but little. The keel of our boat came in contact with the bottom many times, therefore, we were obliged to shift from larboard to starboard repeatedly. Most every hotel in this country employ runners and you have no idea of the number of

THE HURDY-GURDY HOUSE, VIRGINIA, MONTANA. Page 480.
SUCH A SIGHT IN NEW ENGLAND WOULD SHOCK
THE SENSIBILITIES OF THE WHOLE LAND.

these pestiferous people that beset your path at any landing. Each one holding out his fine accommodations, convenient locality, "splendid table," "cheap fare," etc., etc.

The next day I took the stage and rode thirty miles into the country but not liking the looks of things, returned to Sacramento. Here I remained a week, working one day for which I received the pretty little sum of six dollars. Wouldn't that elevate a person's head in America, where he could board for fifty cents per day? Sacramento in time will be a very large place. It is laid out in squares with broad streets all parallel. Spear and I walked up and down the streets and thought we never saw a better assortment or handsomer stock of goods than the merchants have there. Boston seemed to be transferred to this place.

Next we went to Stockton and only remained one night, proceeding directly to Sonora, a distance of one hundred and twenty miles. Here I remained six weeks and then went to see my brother in Calaveras County, thirty miles from Stockton. I spent a week with my brother and concluded to visit my cousin

THE STEAMER *SENATOR* CARRIED HORACE 160 MILES FROM SAN FRANCISCO TO SACRAMENTO.

PHOTOGRAPH COURTESY OF WELLS FARGO BANK HISTORY ROOM, SAN FRANCISCO

at this place. Owing to my financial affairs, I concluded to foot it back to Sonora, but I happened to get a chance to ride to Stockton on a mule team. I accepted it and had only seventy miles to walk.

I took my valise on my back, only weighing eighteen pounds, and the first day I made thirty miles. The road passed over a broad and expansive plain sparingly studded with large oaks. The soil was very dark and seemed once to have been mud or the bed of a large lake. When I emerged from the Plain, I descended in terraces and they had the appearance of being washed by the water, and even the little pebble stones showed that they had been washed to and fro. In many places there was a high ledge rising some forty or fifty feet above the level of the plain and about every ten feet rise on the ledge, it was worn in and probably done by the rushing of water. Each concavity was formed by the receding of the water which seemed to have remained stationary for a long length of time. But these are my

WALKING TO AGUA
FRIO ON TRAILS MADE
BY INDIANS AND BEASTS.

ideas without raising my right hand! However, I was so much pleased at the sight that I used to sit down and look and gaze and wonder and think how the water covered this earth and what Mr. Conant said in Sabbath School and, in fact, almost forgot where I was. I travelled over forty miles on this plain and then entered a mountainous country. Well, the second day at half past two, I had made twenty-three miles when my feet became so sore, though I bathed them frequently, that I was obliged to take the stage and ride the remainder—seventeen miles. This ended this excursion, pleasant and interesting, though if little Fitz had been with me my burden would have been much lighter.

Charlie, I don't think we would have advanced ten miles per day, because we should have had so much to look at and talk about. Several times I took out my autograph book and pondered over my past life. Among the most striking pieces written there was Marie's. Nothing could come truer to pass than the sentiment expressed in her few lines. Here it is:

> "Go make thy home
> In some desert place,
> Which no voice may gladden,
> No foot steps grace."

The reason of that selection was on account of the piece posted in the cover you remember! In reading these over and thinking of the associations connected with them, it rather made me feel despondent, but I would cheer up and think of the "better days coming."

By the way, let me remark that Spear and I were together all the time till I went to see my brother and since then only a few days. Your opinion of Spear was not exactly correct. He is a very worthwhile fellow, full of fun, makes a good appearance and as sincere as anybody, but still he is good-hearted and accommodating and willing to do what is right, though rather easily influenced, and not dissipated or reckless to my knowledge. Or he is not now. All the time I was with him he was just as steady as I was and I think I could pass for a Pilgrim anywhere. His worst immoral habit was profanity, and that I spoke to him about every day till I nearly broke him of it. We made a solemn agreement not to contract any vices in California, let the temptations be few or many. Well, I remained in Sonora three days and then started for Agua Frio. Spear was at work there at a hotel, but since has gone to mining.

A few words about Sonora. Sonora is a City, but why is what my wisdom never could conjecture. It is laid out in every conceivable way. It is situated between two parallel hills north and south of a transverse ridge of a low elevation. It is in the center of one of the best mining districts in California, hence there is much gambling going on, for where the mines are most productive, there iniquity is the most prevalent. There is one French woman that gambles in the "Long Tom" who has made over forty thousand dollars already and says that when she gets ten more she is going to stop. She employs five or six men. Every day they help her pursue her honorable occupation. This "Long Tom" is a gambling house. It is fifty feet wide and two hundred feet long and all occupied as a gambling house. Spear and I have stood in the middle of the building and tried to converse when they were betting right smart, but the din and noise arising from the changing of money made it almost impossible. Such a sight in New England would shock the sensibilities of the whole land.

Well, I will get along. You have seen enough of Sonora. I left Sonora at nine o'clock and before the sun went down I reached Don Pedro's Bar, a distance of twenty five miles. My route was mostly by trails. There are thousands of trails in this country made by the Indians and wild beasts. A trail is merely a foot path. Here I stayed all night and the next day I reached Bear Valley, thirty miles. Hereafter, I will speak of my journey from Don Pedro's Bar to Bear Valley. At nine o'clock the next day I reached Agua Frio and found my cousin.

I JOIN MY BROTHER ON AGUA FRIO CREEK IN MARIPOSA COUNTY.

April 4th. Tomorrow I am obliged to go to Mariposa, having been summoned as a juror. I endeavored to avoid being called upon but the sheriff caught me and there is no doing otherwise. The miners are determined not to go if they can possibly help it, as they get nothing for pay. As soon as they see an Officer coming, the shovels drop very quick and such running and skulking would beat the Indians. You see there were four of us in a store when the Sheriff rode up and we all made for the back door but he was right after us. I got within about four feet of a large hole when he saw me and screams, "Your name, Sir, the man with a red shirt," and kept right on after the others, but he only caught two of us, two running around one side of the store and two the other. I have been summoned twice before this as a Juryman, but have only sat once. Now you must excuse me till I do a little courting, though I hope I shall not form any "entangling alliances!"

SHERIFF SUMMONING A JUROR . . . SUCH RUNNING AND SKULKING WOULD BEAT THE INDIANS.

April 5th. Well, Charlie, I am done *courting*! I found no one that could reciprocate my affection, consequently, came home. My name was called but happened to be twenty-fifth man and as they only wanted twenty-four, I was excused. I was right smart glad for it would have been twenty dollars out of my pocket to have remained. Allowing I had as much money! Small gains with a large aggregate will be my motto.

In writing this letter I am somewhat at a loss to know how to commence again. I have so much to write and cannot write it all this time that it rather confuses me. I think I have rather a joke on Helen. She says she thinks as "much of me now as ever she did!" Well, I am going to write to her that I don't doubt that but the question in my mind is "Did she ever think anything of me?" I shall be very serious in speaking of this and also my heart. I like Helen first rate. She was very good company and always seemed very honest. You didn't see Jennie's note, did you? Capital, Sir! Worth a farm down East. Jennie was one of my particular favorites but I always avoided letting her know it so as to retain her acquaintance.

Truly, my pleasures come not single. Today, I received five letters, making twenty-four pages—and among the rest was yours of December 30th. I haven't the ability to express my thanks to you for your kindness in favoring me with so much satisfaction. In the position that I am in it seems the greatest pleasure I ever enjoyed is to receive a good letter from an Old Friend. From a person whom I more than respected. Though I did not make any definite arrangement with you concerning correspondence, yet you have done better by me than all of my friends put together. Stephens agreed to answer any letter that I would write him, being in common sympathy. I agreed to write him once a month, expecting that he would answer them as punctual. But what has come to pass? Not an answer yet! Four months after my first letter I stopped and have not written since. Spear tells me he received a letter from Stephens dated Feb. 14th, in which he mentioned the reception of one from me dated Jan. 1st. Four long letters did I write him and time has elapsed sufficient for the answers of them all. Please give him my regards and say that I am any way but pleased with his promises. Perhaps he has not received mine, and perhaps he has, and perhaps they have been answered and are detained, and perhaps if this is the case all will be right. Every person that I write to or have written to since leaving Boston, I have noted down so that I know just when my letter is due. This is my 70th letter since I left Boston for California and only once before this have I written to little Fitz. My conscience is smitten but if I live and be healthy, I will try and make ample amends. Seems as though I could sit right where I am and fill twenty-four sheets to you and then not tell you half what I think. My head seems a pint with a bushel running in. I shall omit a description of mining and our cabin till next mail, in which I shall positively write.

You speak of "observing the Sabbath" and with much feeling. In regards to myself, I am just as strict an observer of the Sabbath as I used to be. I never have worked an hour on the Sabbath in California, nor ever attended places of amusement or practiced visiting gambling houses. It is almost impossible to attend church on account of their scarcity and locality. The last meeting I attended was in a bar room. Verily, this seemed like bearding the lion in his den. Drinking and swearing was

A BAR ROOM
BECAME THE
MEETING HOUSE
ON SUNDAY.

the order, before meeting and after. The Northern people as a general thing observe the Sabbath, but the Southerners make but little difference. More intoxication, more fighting and more disturbance on the Sabbath than any other day in the week. I have the name of being the steadiest person on the creek. I have, at several times, tasted liquor but took it as a medicine and not for the pleasure or honor. I am called small and low-down because I will not drink and treat. The standard of a whole soul here is his liberality in treating. I seldom leave my cabin except on business.

As regards reading, I improve every opportunity I get. My literary food is mostly papers, there being but a few books in the county of a sensible nature. People here have a perfect mania for reading novels. I began to notice this the moment I landed on the Isthmus. Nearly every man seemed to have one in his pocket. The only book that I have bought in this country is a dictionary! I buy a Tribune and Boston Journal every steamer. They are only fifty cents apiece.

OUR NEWSPAPERS ARE A MONTH OR TWO OLD AFTER TRAVELING BY SHIP, THEN PANAMA MULE AND THEN ABOARD SHIP AGAIN, ON A RIVERBOAT AND FINALLY ON A STAGECOACH TO MARIPOSA.

I sent to San Francisco for your letter by express, the regular price being one dollar. I was four times rewarded for the expense. I enclose in this letter two specimens of gold and a few flowers. They are not what I could send you but they are all that I am willing to trust through the agent of Uncle Sam. O, I forgot to tell you that I have bought me a Spanish dictionary, grammer and spelling book. I am trying to learn something of the Spanish language. My brother can talk Spanish very well now. I write this mail to Mother, Sister, Helen, Jennie, and you; therefore, I must bring it to a close in order to do justice to them. Be patient, you will get this the middle of May and hereafter I will write much oftener. I would have written this on two sheets had it not been for the flowers and gold.

From your Friend, Friend
Horace

Charlie — Direct mail to Agua Frio

[14]

LETTER 2

Plea From A Bookworm

Agua Frio, April 11, 1854

Charlie:

As it is impossible for me to go to Mariposa before this mail closes, I shall send a letter to you by the Pacific Express Company Nicaragua Line, one week later, which will be found at Adams & Co., Boston, containing some money and if you will do me the favor to subscribe for the papers mentioned, I will endeavor to have a small surplus left for your trouble. Why I send by express is that you may receive the money before leaving Massachusetts. And provided that you are not there, perhaps your Father would do the business in Boston and you could enclose Bank Notes for those out of the State. There is no such thing as Bank Bills here. Not safe to send coin. The papers in Boston will be the Telegraph, Journal, Post - political - Ballou's Pictorial & Waverly Magazine and some other one. However, the letter which I shall send will give full particulars. - - As Helen P. says, the above looks "horrible."

Yours truly,
Horace

NB
Cleared off this morning.

From an old lithograph by "Quiro & Co."   MARIPOSA CITY.   1852

MARIPOSA CITY 1852
FROM AN OLD LITHOGRAPH BY "QUIRO & CO."

LETTER 3

Housekeeping By The Creek

Agua Frio, April 20th, 1854

Dear Charlie Again:

Although my last epistle has not reached its destination, yet, when it arriveth it bringeth you word of another soon after, therefore, this will endeavor to discharge the obligation. I have thought many times since sending the last that you would need a key in order to decipher the contents, but, knowing the principle of self-reliance—as in Arithmetic, Algebra, etc.—I refrain at present, though it may not "discipline your mind" a tithe as much as confuse your ideas.

This letter will only reaffirm what the other has said in regard to my health. I am more contented every day and begin to feel like one of the "old inhabitants." Yesterday it rained very hard all day: much harder than I ever saw it before in all my life. This we know is owing to the warm temperature of the climate. The vapor condenses faster. This morning I rose very early—before light—and went "prospecting" or what you would call "mineralizing." I returned before breakfast and picked up $1.50 worth of gold. The rain washing the dirt from the gold makes it very easy to find. Wouldn't you like to live in a country where the loam and gravel contained a sprinkling of the precious "ore" so that you could go out after a shower and pick up little pieces? No doubt, you would! How much I have wished you were here to go on these little excursions with me. Pecuniarially, I should be loath to give you one half or go in company for I presume I could find twice as much or see a much smaller piece. It requires some practice, as well as good sight, to be sharp in finding gold. However, come out here and you shall have half we find! Bring some good works on geology and what we don't learn—ahem—won't be worth knowing!

EVERYTHING HAS A VERY SOLEMN LOOK.

Well, Charlie, now I will tell you where I am sojourning. Our camp is located in Mariposa County, the extreme southern part of the mines, just about half way between the Coast Range and Sierra Nevadas. I ascended a hill a short distance from our cabin the other day and there I could behold the snow-capped mountains of Sierra Nevada pointing far into the heavens and also the low dark dingy coast range stretching as far as the eye could reach. It was the most beautiful sight I ever saw, barring the view from Mt. Washington. My Brother and Cousin accompanied me and there we remained for several hours almost carried away by the scenery. One peculiarity of the mountains in this vicinity is that they are covered with grass to the very summit, with now and then a clump of oak that gives the appearance of large orchards at a distance. Everything seems to have a very solemn look and everything looks new and strange. Even the heavens have the appearance of a new zenith. The moon is almost directly over my head and when new, forms nearly a perfect basin, the north cant being a little the highest. You know in America when the Indian can hang the powder horn on the moon it is a sign of rain but here the moon will hold a large quantity of water and the sign exactly the reverse.

THE
ADVANTAGE
OF MULE
POWER.

But I am departing from my dissertation. You can travel almost anywhere with a mule and roads are constructed with but little expense. Agua Frio lies between two ranges of hills running nearly southeast and northwest. What latitude this place is in I am unable to tell but it is a considerable south of San Francisco. So much for locality. And now for circumstances.

I am living in an old fashioned log cabin about twelve by fifteen feet. It is very secure against any enemy, being built up of large logs and well mossed. We have only one door and one window to our rustic mansion, choosing darkness rather than light, you see. The internal arrangements are very tasty, myself having the control. As I told Jennie, our cabin is divided into two parts, inside and out. The inside being all in one room and also the out. What we lose here in one point we gain in another. Now, in America, you use wood for floors, which decays and has to be repaired, but we have a slab from Mother Earth, durable and always in its place. Somehow or other our patent. stove happens to be a huge fire place. How pleasant it seems to build up a right smart fire and all get up in front of it and talk over old times. The most interesting part of my life seems a blank, for the reason that I have no one that has been connected with it to talk with. Our window is a small trap door which we use as a cat hole. In stead of reposing on soft down, we rest our weary limbs on a piece of canvas attached to two poles. Woolen blankets are our bed clothes. Everything in our cabin is just as handy as can be. Each one has his own space and a place to put his own things. My brother and I do the cooking, taking turns by the week. I tell you, Charlie, I am getting to be a great cook! I made some biscuits tonight that would almost sail in the air, so light! I baked them in the coals in an iron kettle. We had for supper warm biscuit and custard, both of which I made. Once a week we fry about a half bushel of doughnuts and a lot of turnovers. Pewter plates, iron spoons, and tin dippers compose our china ware. Our domestic family consists of four hens, one dog, and a cat. The dog keeps thieves away nights; the cat takes care of the rats and mice and the hens furnish us with eggs; therefore, you see, we have something for them all to do. Eggs usually are three dollars per dozen, though now only one and a half. Taking things all into consideration, we are getting to be quite independent. Own a house, barn, some stock, plenty of land, and all the wild animals we can catch. Oh, how I wish the distance was such that you could come and see me and spend some vacation! Plenty to eat, drink, wear, and sport with. I work all day mining in the mud and water and feel just like a Boy of twenty-two at night.

By the way, you wish some light upon the different modes of mining. I will try and tell what I am capable of, though I fear you will be more confused than instructed. First, I will speak about the Gold. We have three kinds of gold; virgin, washed and lead. Virgin gold appears to have been thrown out or separated from the rock and never been moved since, it being very porous and rough. This gold is mostly found in gulches and high banks. Washed gold is very fine, resembling flour and scaly. It is mostly found in the creeks among the sand and gravel. I would say that virgin gold is mostly in the loam and washed dirt. Lastly, lead gold is most always found in the ledges where it is soft and slaty. This gold seems to have been thrown out of the earth by some internal convulsion and runs along in one direction for a great many rods. Some times a strip of ledge two feet wide will pay ten dollars to the square foot for

AN OLD FASHIONED LOG CABIN—DIVIDED INTO TWO PARTS, INSIDE AND OUTSIDE. I WORK ALL DAY MINING IN THE MUD AND WATER.

a great ways and you go a foot either side of the strip and you can't get the colour. This is why they call it lead gold, because it confines itself to so narrow a space. This gold is very coarse, heavy and smooth. There are several other minor kinds such as quartz gold, black gold, etc., but they are found among the other kinds. The manner of finding gold is very simple, though there are as many ways as there are miners. However, they all come under the same principle. I will tell you our mode now and in some other epistle explain different ones. For description see small slip.

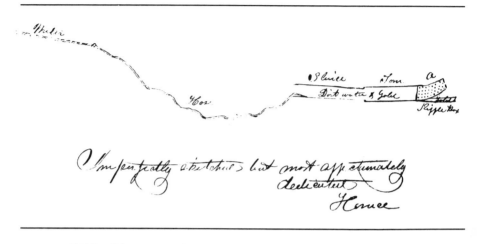

"IMPERFECTLY SKETCHED BUT AFFECTIONATELY DEDICATED."

HORACE

Our Tom and Sluices are set in a similar position, as indicated. The dirt and gravel is thrown into the sluices and in course of time get down to "A." "A" is a sheet of iron perforated with holes and fastened to the lower end of the Tom. A man stands at "A" with a square pointed shovel and works the stones and gravel over this iron till clean and then throws them away, the small pebbles, dirt and gold going through into the Riffle Box. This box is the same width as the Tom and about four feet long. As soon as the gold passes into the Riffle Box it settles right to the bottom and there remains, being so very heavy. We have the Riffle Box so much inclined that there is not only about an inch of dirt on the surface, our object being to get the gold to the bottom as soon as possible. The stones thrown away by the man at "A" are called the "Headings" and those that pass through the Tom iron "Tailings." Last epistle I enclosed to you two specimens of gold. Trust you received them.

...ch in dirt that there is not only about one inch of dirt on the surface, your object being to get the gold to the bottom as soon as possible. The stones thrown away by the Miner is a pile called the "Henchrey's" and stone that pass through the Tom can screenings Tom

Last month I sent you two specimens of gold, true are you them?

Our Tom and Sieve are cut in a similar form and gravel is thrown in to the Sieves and in course of the A. A. is a list of iron fragments with hole and ... the Tom. A man stands at a with a square pointer and gravel over this iron till clean and then throws away dirt and gold going through is to the Ripple box. ... the Tom and about your Tom long. As soon as the gold found it settles right to the bottom and then remain being a very heavy the Tom the box

Charlie, I am under the necessity of closing. I intended to have written as much more this evening but my brother fails to write home—unavoidably—and I deem it my duty to write them. I did not write Jennie last mail but have two sheets written this. Soon I will give you plenty of marks and show my disposition whether interesting or not. I am much troubled about writing, having many callers and no accommodations. Give my love to Stephens and tell him I will be as forebearing and lenient as possible. Nothing from him yet. Also give my regards to John Marsh and tell him I should be highly gratified to answer a letter from him. When you read this keep my disposition in mind.

Press on, Charlie, till you possess the oratorical prowess of Demosthenes and the philosophical genius of Franklin. If you should write, direct it to Sonora. I shall go there shortly.

Yours forever,
Horace

LETTER 4

Yearning For Mail

Agua Frio, June 23rd, 1854

Dear Charlie:

In a very few minutes I must write all that circumstances will admit. By this mail I send to you or to your care, some quartz specimens. The name upon each paper enclosed around the specimens is to whom I intended it to be given. I don't wish you to put yourself out to distribute them, but wait till some convenient time. They are not what I would like to have sent but the best that I could obtain now. I have distributed them as well and impartial as I could and hope they will be so received. They are from Mariposa County, California. One thing I wish you to state, particularly when giving or sending them, and that is not to attach my name to the specimen. Instead of being Agua Frio—which shows my hurry, I am in Sonora. I came here the 15th and shall remain till the 26th and then return to the Old Log Cabin in Agua Frio, where I intend to remain for one year. I intended to have written you a long letter from this place but it is almost impossible. When I get back to the cabin I will make amends. I also send you by this mail a Chinese paper. Knowing that you have a love for the curious and think some of studying the languages, I thought that a perusal of this might enable you to succeed faster in some other. Probably at first you will not understand very readily but after a short time the difficulty in a measure will be obviated!! Last mail I received a letter from Helen and the mail before one from

Clara—both admirable letters, particularly Clara's. Charlie, I wish you would find out—unsuspectingly—why Stephens doesn't write me. With regret I close. Health good.
    Remember Snow   Write immediately

                              Yours very truly
                                Horace

LETTER 5

Baked Beans
And Old Bones

Agua Frio, July 24th, 1854

Dear Charlie:

After a visit of twenty-two days at Sonora, I returned to the good old Log Cabin in good health and spirits. My first business after getting washed up and something to eat was to go to the post office and to my gratification, after arriving, I found a good long interesting letter from you bearing date of May 11th and also two others. I returned home as soon as possible and seated myself in the easiest position possible, for I was very tired, having travelled over twenty miles before this— and commenced on "Little Fitz's letter." I think you understand the art of letter writing to a charm for I never have received one yet without wishing there was more and still your letters are of an uncommon length to what mine average. My last epistles have been very hasty and without much thought, for which you must excuse, and for the future I will write regularly with more news. Sometimes I can sit down and write three or four pages without any hesitation and comparatively quick, but as a general thing I have to spend much time, so much so that sometimes I get all out of patience and close very abruptly. This, I suppose, is owing to small language and a dull brain, which I possess to a wonderful degree. But as "practice makes perfect," I have some hopes of improving. I am glad that you were so fortunate in obtaining a situation but I think that I would rather see your letters dated Harvard

College or Brown University or some such place, for "though small but desperate," you have faculties that only need developing to place you in some eminent position. I might attend school two score and odd years and never get only about so far, for I haven't that "progressive principle" in me which is necessary to become a good scholar. But you say, "try, never give up, persevere," and so do I, for here lies the secret of what little I do know. But I'll pass this, as I never thought of writing in this manner when I commenced.

I COOK DOUGHNUTS, TURN-OVERS, BREAD, BISCUITS, BEANS, AND FLAPJACKS . . . WHAT AN ACCOMPLISHED YOUNG MAN I SHALL BE.

By the way, when I commenced this epistle, I commenced cooking some beans and now I have them parboiled and pork in, all ready for baking; therefore, I shall not be disturbed for a short time. You see, I am learning several lessons that you will not get at the Traveller Office. Only think of working all day, going home at night, rolling up your sleeves, making biscuits, doughnuts, flap jacks, frying pork or ham, washing dishes and all such things as pertain to domestic duties! Curious life to live, isn't it, Charlie? What an accomplished young man I shall be when I return.

We are now throwing up dirt for next winter. I will explain to you—The gold, as a general thing, is below the loam in the gravel and on top of the ledge, so we throw off the loam and throw the gravel and ledge up in piles. Then, you see, next winter we can wash much faster and use the water to a better advantage. We commence work in the morning, always having our breakfast cooked night beforehand—invariably before sunrise, and work till ten, then lay off till about three and work till seven. We have gotten to be a very little independent; therefore, we work just as we choose. If we choose to sit down, we do it and nobody says, "why do you so." If we choose to quit at nine or at five, we do it and take our ease. We have a very large awning that we hoist over us and work in the cool shade. But, to satisfy you that it is cool in the shade, I will tell you that the thermometer stands from 104° to 119°!! I never knew what excessive heat was till I came here. Some people make them a bed close to the brook and whenever they get too warm they roll in and cool off; roll out and sleep till warm again. Do you wonder that people die in California? You will see by our mode of work that I have plenty of time to spend and write, and perhaps think that I ought to write better letters but where a persons talents are so limited as mine, there is no need of remarks. But what I was going to say was that I improve every hour.

My Brother and I purchased in Sonora over twenty dollars worth of books, which we now have in our cabin. These are a few of the books—one grammer, one arithmetic, one work in physiology, one in phrenology, Pictorial description of the United States, Mental Philosophy, the American Manual, one Dictionary, History of Wonderful Inventions, Year Book of Facts, one book on Chemistry, How to Become an Actor, History of Horses, Origin of Government, besides several others of smaller note. We bought no novels or "two bit" trash, nothing but what would be useful. I never sit down nor lie down in the daytime without a book in my hand. My brother is camping with me or we are camping together and work together. This seems good but the better part of my life having been spent in Massachusetts, I miss a Bay State companion as much as I would a Brother. Of course, those things which are past in the memory are the most pleasant topics to talk about. All things that we were acquainted with in common ceased five years ago, and all transactions since he is no company at all; that is in a small degree.

While at work last Thursday we found a very "curious Specimen." We first came upon some little bones and not knowing what they were, we dug very carefully around them and, taking one bone out after another, we had before us in a few minutes, the Skeleton of a human being! You can imagine our surprise as we removed the dirt and there before us was the mortal remains of some poor being. He was buried about five feet under ground and facing the East. There were no signs or traces of a grave around it and the dirt directly over it was just as hard as the adjoining. Who put the body there and when it was done, no one knows, not even the "Oldest Inhabitant." The physician in our place—who by the way is an excellent scholar—says they could not have been there less than thirty years. By the bones it must have been a man, and a very large one, too, for by putting the frame together, it was one six feet

WHO DID IT? THE BEAR?

long. I improved the opportunity of examining these bones and learned more respecting the machinery or workings of the System than I could by books and diagrams in several terms. I had just enough theory to take a ready view of all the parts, for they were very well preserved, being buried in a place very dry and free from moisture. Everyone who examined the skeleton says the skull is the one of a white man and this adds more to the mystery, for the first white man that ever settled upon the creek—1849—is living here now and he never saw or heard anything concerning it. It is quite laughable to hear the miners speculate concerning the mystery. Some rather thought that he came here on a "prospecting tour" and sunk a hole and not finding the "colour" laid down in the hole and died a sensible and quiet death! Others thought that he might have been one of the Hudson Bay Company who was in quest of furs and dug a hole to entrap a Grizzly but, unhappily, got caught himself. But the sensible portion of the community thought his death and burial was prior to the reign of Solomon. The skull can be seen by calling at our cabin, which we hope you will avail yourself of the opportunity.

Your friend,
Horace

July 25, 1854
My bake beans are splendid. Would that you were here to eat some. Eat some out of a *tin plate*, with an iron spoon. How much better they would relish them eaten from nice china ware and from a table loaded down with the edibles, the fragrance, all of which rush upon the olfactory nerves, thus destroying the flavor of "my good bake bread!" Think of me when you eat bake beans. Enclosed in this letter is a sheet showing a few scenes in a miner's life. The "Night in a Log Cabin" is capital and reminds me of Bridgewater. I presume he is playing my favorite tune or something pertaining to old Boz. Do you remember the night Mary brought in the cake? Wasn't that a treat? How much I do think of Bridgewater, think of the good times I enjoyed there, and the bad ones. By the way, I received a letter from Clara a few weeks since. Don't hardly know what to think of it. Clara wrote me a first-rate letter and, indeed, I was surprised to think she could do so well. It was well arranged, well written, and well composed, so much so that it rather puts me in the shade. These are the things that cause me reflection: "write often," "your daguerrotype," "a lock of hair"!!!

Now, Charlie, betwixt you and I and the rest of man-kind, I don't wish to get into any "entangling alliances." Because of many reasons, and I am afraid if I correspond, as requested, that there will be something else in the wind than oxygen and nitrogen, by and by. What shall I do? compromise and preserve my dignity, or pray for Old Lang Syne? A few suggestions from you would be thankfully received, as you are more experienced in these things!!! However, I shall write—reserved—again, and see what will come to pass.

Then there is that Stephens! In my next letter I must tell you about how this important personage and I stand. I have waited for a letter from him till my patience has ceased to be a virtue and he and I now, unless his excuse is nearly divine, are two separated persons.

I have read much about your *suit* in the good City of Boston and think you had a right smart time of it. What awful creatures these Abolitionists are! I should think the patriotic pro-slavery people would move out of the Union and leave them! I suppose this excitement had but little to do with you in your official capacity. Nor would any such scenes. Please tell me what your principal business is. You mentioned of sending me some papers, but woe be to Uncle Sam! None have come yet, but I must speak more fully of these things next time. Well, Charlie, with these few lines composed and written as they are, I shall be over the principal necessity of submitting to perusal. Painful, because of the failure to answer your epistle, which was so interesting. It is now time to commence work.
P.M.—and this has got to go to the Post office tonight or remain over. We live one and a fourth mile from the Post office, which makes a very fast walk there and back.

Well, I have been there five times and back, of course, and not get a thing. Don't you suppose I wished my friends the other side of Jordan! Well, keep your eye open tight, Charlie, and learn all you can to tell Snow when he comes home. I hope you have received those specimens that were sent from Sonora before this. Here I go with the perspiration dropping quite fast.

I am, exp.

Horace

Please tell me where you board, whether at home or not, and where to direct your letters.

H.

LETTER 6

Pangs Of Homesickness

Agua Frio, August 7th, 1854

Dear Charlie:

Would that I could wield the pen like a Byron to express my thankfulness for your remembrance of me in the form of a letter, two papers, and Horace Mann's address, which were mailed July 4th and arrived in Agua Frio August 2nd. Although I wrote you a few lines last mail, yet I cannot allow this one to leave without sending a few words, however void of interest. The mail which arrived the middle of July brought me nothing and this one which arrived the first of August brought me nothing excepting from "Little Fitz." Have my correspondents deserted me? Are my letters of such a character and composition that they are not worth answering? Or am I of so little consequence that it is not necessary to notice me whatever my claims may be? I have kept an account of every letter written in California, when mailed and to whom addressed and this epistle—if it may be called one—is my 97th. In regard to the answers, when I receive one I immediately check the same in my book, so that I have debt and credit readily at view. In looking over my account, I find fourteen delinquent correspondents who never have written me at all and some of them I wrote four letters before closing and on an average, two apiece. Adding to them some twenty odd more who are a little dilatory, and I have over fifty unanswered letters. Do you suppose that Snow—that "sensitive mortal," will forget all this? I know that we should do as we would be done by but the exceptions to all

[33]

rules justifys in this case. Nearly every one of these persons shook me by the hand and said faithfully that they would answer all that I could write. *"May they escape the penitentiary."*

As I told you in the last that I would explain to you concerning Stephens and myself, I will occupy a few more minutes and then leave my grievances for the concensus thereof when they shall be sensible of it. You are aware that Stephens

OUR EVENINGS
ARE THE MOST
BEAUTIFUL I
EVER SAW.

and I were *victims to the same folly,* and a sympathy of feeling should spring up between us attaching one another, no one would doubt. I wrote him five letters in good faith and laid the blame onto Uncle Sam for answers till reason told me better. Excuse the digression and you shall have enough more matter to make amends.

I am very sorry that all your favorites are emigrating to the State of Matrimony! Helen to be married soon and Jennie engaged!! What is the world coming to? How much pleasure and regret my Normal career does afford me. However, I formed but few acquaintances that will be lasting, though as long as some of the girls remain single, I shall have some affinity for them. I suppose to return there two years hence would be like visiting a strange school.

One year ago the second day of last month was the last time that I beheld Bridgewater. How quick the time has passed. How plainly I can see the cars approaching, see Spear upon the platform, hear him turn a deaf answer to allowing me to remain over, see the platform crowded with scholars, hear the engine begin to puff, see the depot and crowd in the distance and realize Snow embarked on an unknown voyage. How long will it be before I shall see Old New England again?

Our evenings here are the most beautiful I ever saw. The atmosphere is free of moisture so much so that clothing washed after sundown will be perfectly dry before morning. Well, I have me a bunk erected outdoors to lie on in the evening and many a one have I fallen asleep while thinking about past life in the "Land of Shawmut."

We are still throwing up dirt and feel very confident that our labor will be rewarded next winter. This forenoon we washed a pan taken from a small crevice and obtained $5.30. Our ground will pay by no means at this rate, but it shows that there is gold

(EARLY MINING SCENE PUBLISHED BY JAMES MASON HUTCHINGS.)

in it and gives us courage to persevere. We only "prospect" enough to pay our way so as not to fall behind hand. This mail I send you some mining scenes and sketches in a pamphlet

[35]

which you will find quite amusing. Literature of an instructive character is very scarce here and particularly on newspapers, which are on a very low order. I have read Mr. Mann's speech and cannot praise it in too high terms. I am a thousand times obliged to you for your kindness and will show it in a different way by and by.

Remember me to Mrs. T's folks. Keep your eye on the North Star and now and then think of Snow.

Yours as ever,
Snow.

"CALIFORNIA NEWSPAPERS ARE ON A VERY LOW ORDER."

HOWEVER, THEY KEPT THE MINERS INFORMED AND ENTERTAINED.

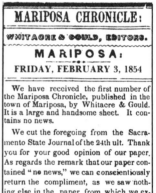

LETTER 7

Spirit Of Liberty

Agua Frio, August 19th, 1854

Dear Charlie:

I was happily not disappointed the other day in finding your letter of June 17th in Agua Frio. I obtained it the day I put my last to you in the office. I left Sonora July 7th and probably it arrived there about the 16th. Though I was in possession of July 2nd, yet this was just as acceptable. I regret the mistake more on your account than mine, for I would gladly have attempted an answer had it come to hand. I am glad that you think of writing every mail, for I had much rather have four pages twice a month than six or eight once in four weeks. An interval of four weeks between communications seems very long, especially if the correspondence is entertaining. As your business is such that writing will soon become rather monotonous, I will only ask four pages once a fortnight, but you must bear with me if I should occasionally add a little more. I love to write as well as most any other person but, unfortunately, have a poor faculty of interesting the addressed. I have written many letters in this country that were severe tasks because the promise was forced from me, and not voluntarily, but when I write to a person who I think is a *friend* and does as he would like to be done by, then it is a pleasure. For every letter I put in the post office to such a person, I feel just so much the happier. This is only demonstrating the great truth that it is better to "give than to receive." I begin to realize in you, Charlie, a *Friend*, something that I cannot affirm of another school mate or associate in the world and I trust it may continue and be profitable as long as we live. Pledges of faith and friendship receive a severe test in twelve months and if there be an *Arnold* among them, you are sure to know it. Had I been some Ancient Knight and my professed *friends standard bearers*, I should have had but one man to bear the colours and in all probability been a captive in the enemy's camp before now. But I will talk of something else.

You think perhaps that my sentiments or "private prejudices" were partly removed against the "peculiar institution" after visiting Norfolk? Not a particle, Charlie. I am more out and out an Abolitionist than ever. What little I saw in Norfolk doubly convinces me of the enormity of that horrid institution. Norfolk is in a complete state of delapidation. The buildings were old, all tumbling to pieces, out of repair, ill contrived, grass growing in the streets, every other house a grog shop and everybody destitute of energy, learning and good morals.

I became quite sociable with one person, who by his air and manners seemed well provided for in this world and he told me that slavery was the greatest curse that ever befell this country. I asked him what the leading pursuit of the inhabitants was in Norfolk. And, says he, "Indolence." Says he, "We have no public schools, no public libraries, no scientific institutions, nothing that tends to elevate the moral or mental faculties of the people." He told me that a few years ago some Boston capitalists came there and purchased four acres of land adjoining the beach, intending to erect some wharves and storehouses and carry on a mercantile business in the "Old Dominion," but, says he, "when the fact became known to the citizens, they were so enraged that they proceeded to the house of the land owner and by threats of violence forced him to rescind the bargain and declare that no such system of humbuggery should be established in that city. While we were talking this very time a gentleman passed through the room and, says my friend, "There! that person owns more real estate than any other man in the city, and after deducting the taxes and repairs he has hardly enough left to give him a decent support."

At the time I was there the papers were discussing the *propriety* of adopting the *Common School system* and the press was equally divided. Those who opposed it based their arguments upon the saying that a "Little knowledge was a dangerous thing," and also upon what a celebrated Virginian said once that all the *Light* he wanted his constituents to have was the light of the Sun! The failure of Thomas Jefferson's prediction that Norfolk would be by the middle of the eighteenth century the Commercial emporium of the United States can easily be accounted for.

As I am speaking about slavery, let me tell you something about a Missourian of our place. While I was reading one of your last papers this person, whom we will call Mr. Pike—and by the way, all Missourians are called *Pikes* in this country—came along and wanted to know what they had done with those

Fugitive Slave Act
1848. Mexico ceded California to the United States. **1850.** California requested statehood as a free state but slave-state Senators resisted. The result was the Compromise of 1850, which included the Fugitive Slave Act. Anyone who harbored, assisted or failed to turn in a runaway slave, was penalized. The fugitive could not testify in his own behalf; could not have a jury trial; could be claimed as the property of a slave owner upon presentation of a sworn statement of ownership; and his fate was decided by a federal commissioner, who received $10 if he decided in favor of a slave "owner," $5 if in favor of the slave.

persons engaged in the late Fugitive Slave suit? I told him I did not know and presumed they had not had their trial yet. Then, says Mr. Pike, "Hang 'em; every man ought to be strung right up without judge or jury. What miserable, degraded beings," says he, "they must be!" And then he talked this way for a long time. But what I was coming at was this: In 1850, he started from St. Louis with three yoke of oxen and two slaves for California, intending to work them here for about three years and then sell his cattle and return with the slaves, and also a *Pile* in his pocket, if his plan succeeded; but we'll see. After an expedition across the plains he arrived in California and soon put his slaves and cattle in a fair way to fulfilling his desired plan.

Now, it happened that Mr. Pike came into a country where Yankees abounded and where Yankees abound, there you find an atmosphere impregnated with a small quantity of freedom; I say *small quantity of freedom*, because 30 pieces of silver will work miraculous things nowadays. Well, his slaves inhaled this atmosphere and it wrought wonderful changes upon them, for it is as utterly impossible for a slave to associate with a Yankee and not catch the *Spirit* of Liberty as it is to jump into the water and not get wet. Therefore, his slaves, like Thomas Jefferson, thought, "all men (were) born free and equal" and, consequently, took their departure and told not Mr. Pike which way they went. But the best part of the story is that the slaves thought the oxen ought to have their liberty, besides having great attachment for them, as they had always lived

MR. PIKE LOST HIS SLAVES...
"HE IS TOO LAZY TO WORK,
TOO PROUD TO BEG."

together and accordingly they deserted them not and all went on their way rejoicing, leaving poor Mr. Pike to bake his own beans and earn the money to buy them. Now Mr. Pike is exceedingly wrathful and goes about like a roaring lion with his head full of venom, swearing vengeance upon the Yankees, for he says they are beneath the lowest reptile that creeps on the face of the earth. But, as "barking dogs never bite," no one fears him. At the present time he is about as fit an object for some benevolent institution as I know of. How he lives is a mystery to me, for he is too lazy to work, too proud to beg and not courageous enough to steal. He says the Scriptures never were intended for the Negro race and believes they are entirely exempt from its Commandments! What consistency! By the way, some four months ago Mr. Pike obtained information of the whereabouts of one of his slaves and therefore, by the aid of the blessed Fugitive Slave Law he went in search of his strayed property, and found it, and what do you guess the first thing he did was? Tied the slave up to a tree and gave him a murderous whipping! But what was the consequence? The slave came back with him as submissive as a child, and stayed three nights, but the fourth he assumed business of a very *urgent character* and has not been heard of since! So Mr. Pike is not only minus his slave again, but also the *borrowed* money he spent in reclaiming him.

Now, Charlie, I have taken up much space in speaking about slavery and in order to correspond I shall be obliged to write upon some subjects, for as you are not acquainted with this part of the country, it would be very monotonous to keep writing about old times, and besides, I shall be much more apt to convey something new or worth knowing. Everything that you write is of interest to me because I am acquainted with the parties, but here it is quite different. Now, as our tastes are very different it may be that I have written things to you wholly uninteresting, though not so to me, and to avoid this I would like to have you ask in each letter anything you would wish to know about this country, no matter what, and I will try and inform you as best I can. Such a course as this will be beneficial to us both. Please state what you think of this and make any other such proposals as you think best.

Perhaps, Charlie, you have felt a little slighted because I have not written you more particulars about my future intentions, after you had written me so plainly about yours, but the reason is not because I had not confidence enough in you or wished not to write them, but because I had none to write! I say none to write, but this applies to my return and the *pile* I wish to get. My success last winter is now known in America only by one man, for I never intend my relatives or friends shall know whether I am in good luck or bad, though I wrote them I was out of debt and had money in my pocket. Therefore, this is and always will be—if I can manage it—a secret to them. Now, Charlie, having confidence that you will divulge not, I am going to commence back to my entering the Normal School and tell you all about my financial affairs up to the present time.

Now listen! When I entered the Normal School, I was indebted to my Brother $14, and this was all the demands that there were against me and, moreover, all the monies I were possessed of would not liquidate this small amount at this time. Now it is evident that I was neither an Astor or a Jew. Therefore, I thought if by some honorable means I could become a "Franklin" or "Demosthenes," some future fame must certainly await me. Consequently, through the influence of Mr. Allen, Mr. Plympton guaranteed the required and you find me among the scribes and pedagogues at Bridgewater! Forthwith Mr. P. kindly offered to furnish me with what I should wish and wait two years after graduating for payment. I obtained of Mr. Plympton in all $83.66. $3.66 was for an insurance policy, which I voluntarily had done to secure him. This was just before I visited home. Now, when I returned from Bridgewater the last vacation, I was in need of some clothing and as I was going home, of course, I wanted to look consider-able "kinder slick." Therefore, through the purse of my brother the sum of $20. did the desired thing and Snow went home expecting to cut quite a shine! When I left Bridgewater, I had a little over $20. and this was the money that fared me home and back. Now I have been home, cut my SHINE, have returned to Boston, am no longer a member of the Normal School, have no funds at my command, no inclination to *settle down*, but feel like travelling, feel as though it might improve my health, pocket and perhaps character. Therefore, after many deliberations and consultations, California was thought the most fitting country to tour in and was chosen. Here again the same obstacle met me, i.e., no funds—but by perseverence, the *evil* was acquired and Snow took up his journey into the far-off land. Now, having learned while at Normal how to collect two or more quantities together and how to express an equivalent, I find my indebtedness to be at this time $267., individualized as follows: Mr. P. $83; Brother, $34; George Young, $100; Charles H. Spear, $50. Wasn't that a pretty little sum to accompany a poor, unsophisticated person into such a dissipative country as this? But hush! The worst is not yet. Passing over time and events till the first of January, you will find me in Agua Frio related to the world thus: Mr. P, $83; Brother, $34; George Young, $100; Charles Spear, $100; Mr. Ketton, $27; Mr. Woodward, $28; Total: $372!!! and not a farthing to counter-balance. Passing over events again, till the present time, I mean from January, and, pleasing to relate, the *boot* is on the other foot, just like this: $100 sent to pay Mr. Plympton; $40 checked to Brother; $100 checked to George Y.; $100 paid to Spear; Ketton and Woodward paid. $50 sent to Father, $12.50 to Sister, and furthermore, have got $100 at interest, besides owning one half of a good Cabin and cooking utensils, one half of three claims, the same interest in a good stock of mining tools and other articles too numerous to mention. Now, Charlie, I don't wish to be boisterous or ungentlemanly, but let us throw off a little of our superfluous hilarity and give three cheers for Snow. There now, HURRAH! HURRAH!! HURRAH!!! Therefore, you will see that last winter I placed myself beyond the annoyance of Sheriffs and proved myself worthy of trust, helped my father in his old age, cheered my sister, who was learning the vest-making trade in Boston, laid up $100, and placed myself in a favorable position to do much better this winter. Do you think this was bad, Charlie?

Now, Charlie, for want of space I must stop this subject for this mail and leave you to ponder whether you think Snow has cause to smile or not. In my next, I will commence at San Frisco and tell you how much money I had when I landed, how I managed in Sacramento and finally, how I existed till I commenced in Agua Frio. This will be the most interesting part of my life in California. I laugh every time I think of it.

August 23rd. What a truthful expression that is which says, "Large bodies move slow." The Atlantic mail of July 20th arrived in our town today—though we have had Atlantic news over a week—and what amount of mail matter do you think it brought Snow? Just one paper from *Little Fitz*! Therefore, one month will elapse without hearing anything personal from either friend or foe. But, as I am used to these things, the world will still revolve. I received a short note from Smith the other day dated June 11th and the answer I direct to you, as he would not be in New York in October and wish you to forward it, if agreeable, and, by the way, as it contains nothing secret, I will give you the privilege of reading it. In modesty, it is far above Smith's, but you must make allowances.

I enclose in this letter a two dollar and half piece so that the aggregate of these petty depredations upon your pocket may not be too large. As a favor, I wish you to keep an exact account of all you spend for me and when this is gone, inform me, as of any business transactions. But I will try and keep you in funds without any reminders. Anything that you see or hear of that you think might be interesting to me, please purchase it, I mean in pamphlet form, and forward it. Purchase some literary paper now and then and if you choose, any mail, because a "variety is the spice of life," you know. Pictorial Waverly Magazine and the like would be preferred. I enclose in Smith's epistle a mining sheet for you which is very truthful, especially the miner's weighing their gold. You will observe the table and also the candle and stick. The prospecting miner is possibly going home, as his gold is being shipped. I enclose a wrapper around Smith's letter for privacy on the part of Smith.

My brother sends his regards and thinks you are a boy of some sense. I close as ever, your friend,

Horace C. Snow

LETTER 8

Down On Our Luck

Agua Frio, August 30th, 1854

Dear Charlie:

As delays are dangerous, I commence this early, that you may be more sure of another chapter of Snow's experience. Unlike Smith, my et ceteras will all be itemized so that the mind may not associate tapping boots or cotton hose with the same when the expenditures commence, or as they are taking place. Last mail I enclosed a two and half dollar piece in a letter of eight pages to you which I hope will go direct. I was very careless in doing up the letter to hold the money, but will look out for the future. You ask how my letter came mailed at Frisco and dated Frio. I'll tell you. I was too late for the Agua Frio mail and happening to have a chance to send it by a person who was going home the same time, I availed myself of the opportunity and saved a disappointment. It requires a long-headed, long-winded athletic and mathematical scholar to keep anywhere near up with the arrival and departure of mails. Since July we have had two mails per week, but when they come or go is the puzzle. I always calculate to have my literature in the post office six days previous to the departure at San Francisco. Perhaps some of my letters will not agree with this last statement, but the truth will remain the same. I shall have from now till the tenth to finish, and in the meantime, I expect another epistle from you. Therefore, I will write out my narration before the arrival so as to reply.

Well, to commence, I will say that *the fifth day of September, 1853*, I was in New York and possessed of this world's good: Some baggage, a ticket to California, and exactly $40.

SAN FRANCISCO . . . AND $12.33 IN MY POCKET.

The twelfth day of October, same year, I might have been seen in San Francisco with a convexed valise inwardly and $12.33! Hundreds of people could count their tens of thousands and even millions, but all Snow could show was $12.33! But Snow did not despair. He went to the "Revere of Frisco" Franklin House and ordered a dinner that befitted the occasion. Dinner being over, Snow made his way to a shoe store for he was greatly in want of some shoes, and $1.75 just furnished him with some. Some Natick understandings. Now Snow and his friend Spear perambulated the street and made many inquiries and after a short time held a consultation which resulted in their decision of going to Sacramento the same night. The cause of this hasty departure was the dullness of business and over-population of the city. As the steamer sailed at four o'clock, Snow, with his accustomed punctuality, was on board and as she gracefully moved out of the dock he might have been seen behind a box of goods on the bows taking from his pocket a soiled portmonnaie and counting the skeleton of his former $12.33. How fleeting are the things of this world, thought Snow, when all told only amounted to $2.58. Could it be possible, thought Snow, that I have parted with this much. And he felt in his pockets all over again. That I am reduced to mere nothing before anything was reducable. After a few calculations like these, his mind was tranquil; for dinner, 75 cents; shoes, $1.75; ginger bread, which he had under his arm, 25 cents; ticket to Sacramento, $7; total: $9.75, balance $2.58. At this low water mark of my monetary affairs I will retire, hoping that tomorrow may find the valise convex.

SACRAMENTO . . .
$2.58 IN MY PORTMONNAIE (PURSE).

Morning dawns and Snow finds himself in the streets of Sacramento homeless, and almost moneyless, for as he arrived about three o'clock in the morning he was obliged to purchase a bit worth of cake and a bit worth of coffee to prevent faintness. However, Snow reasoned, he made something here, for he ate no more till noon, thus reducing his pile 25 cents more. Now, Snow, with wonderful sagacity, took $2. from his pocket and firmly enclosed it in his portmonnaie, so that he might know the morrow whereof his bread should come from. Thus leaving him only 33 cents for the remainder of the day. But here Snow's sagacity wasn't so wonderful after all, for he was obliged to pay his night's lodging in advance, which took one-fourth of all his portmonnaie contained. Snow and his companion walked to and fro during the day making many inquiries and holding many consultations and, last of all, in the afternoon they concluded to go to the mines. They conceived that under some old stump or big rock or in some wide crevice or in some high bank, or dormant in some big boulder lay the long-wished for fortune. And of all the creeks and camps and gulches and bars and diggings, Secret Diggings was the one! The very name implies untold sums of gold which only wanted some lucky person to stumble onto it to become a millionaire. Secret Diggings was the place and Secret Diggings they were bound to visit. Already fast horses, long excursions, genteel residences and a handsome wife were in embryo for the future. Therefore, it was resolved that on the morrow they take up their sticks and walk, as the destined place was only 27 miles distant. And also their pockets would be much favored by the operation. In the meantime, all superfluous clothing was disposed of and only such retained as was absolutely necessary. The morning came and what with it? As sure as truth toward evening the day before Snow was attacked with a dysentery and so reduced in the morning that he was unable to walk. What was to be done? Our pile lay in Secret Diggings and must be got, so it was thought best to put Snow aboard the stage, as he thought he was able to ride, and his companion, along with one from Providence, Rhode Island, would come as before. Therefore, Snow took passage, his fare being paid by his friend, who was better supplied in the beginning and which was only $8!!! and soon was in Secret Diggings. The next day at noon his friends were in Secret Diggings and began to hold secret council as to what it was best to do. Here Snow is in the woods respecting his monetary, but will presently emerge in an opening and unfurl his banner. Now it took but a short time for these Down Easters to discover that Secret Diggings was truly Secret Diggings, for if there was ever any gold there, it truly was a secret, for no one had ever found any, or ever expected to. Therefore, in spite of the old teaching, it was resolved to let go of the plow handle and travel back.

Consequently, the third evening from Sacramento found us back again. We returned on a freight wagon at the expense of $1 each. Snow now will emerge from the woods. Just one week and one day from this time, Snow and his companions could be seen in Stockton and all they had between them (for by this time everything had become common) was only $4!!! To return from the arrival of Snow in Sacramento to his arrival in Stockton he had advanced over the left $16!! Divers ways did he manage in Sacramento to save dimes. One meal a day was all he could afford and sometimes none, but he was a very zealous advocate and patronizer of free lunches. At ten in the forenoon and nine in the evening the most fashionable drinking saloons furnished roast beef, pickled cabbage, crackers and cheese, etc., for their patrons, with the expectation that all will step up and take a drink before taking a bite, thus giving permanency to the custom, but Snow, with more *sense* than *cents* at the time, would walk in and carelessly peruse a newspaper or two till a right opportunity afforded and then he would pitch in with a good relish and in the same quiet manner take his exit! thus saving his money and not troubling the proprietor. Two such friendly visits in the forenoon would be sufficient till nine in the evening, for you are aware that gentility and quantity at each place is as much a virtue as moderation while masticating. Therefore, it was necessary to be etiquettical and not partake more than a sufficiency. In the evening Snow usually fared better, as the elements combined in his favor and gave him more confidence. From early morn till dewey eve did Snow in quest of work, but all he could obtain was one day. Had he possessed a chest of tools, he would have been more fortunate, but as he had none, nor any money to buy with, disappointment welcomed him at every application. His companion was more fortunate and obtained work in a boarding house for three days, at the rate of $40 per month. However, the most fortunate part about this was that he was free from expense during this time, the pay being no great gain. Your correspondent, for his day's work, received a sum which nearly astonished him. Never did anything so tickle him or inspire his capabilities as the pay of that day! *SIX DOLLARS* in gold did he receive for that day. Just think! six months a few years before, did he work for $5. per month and one whole year for $7. per month and now, for merely one day, he received $6!! Thought Snow, mathematically, if one day equals one month, what will one year equal? Snow went to the United States Hotel that day and took dinner but fell back on his free lunch in the evening. Perhaps you would like to know what Snow did that day, as it was the first labor he performed in California. It was nothing, more or less, in plain English, than preparing a room to expedite human victims to eternity. In other words, a rum shop. Comments are unnecessary as when you are with the Romans you should do as they do. Though the next morning Snow passed by and was politely asked to take a drink and as politely refused.

Thus, one day after another passed till the afternoon before their departure when they were standing on the levee wondering what their "manifest destiny" was and also observing how beautifully less their funds were growing, when the idea of retrenchment suggested itself to their minds in regards to their lodging, for they had always paid 50 cents per night each and this would suffice them for a day's board. Therefore, it was resolved that they should perambulate in the suburbs and spot a place to repose that night. For they were possessed of some blankets, having exchanged their needless clothing for them. No sooner proposed than they were in the quest of and in a short time an old barn containing a small quantity of straw was chosen about a mile from the levee. About ten o'clock in the evening they repaired thither and rested very well, departing, though, very early. Thus a *Dollar* was saved! The next day, or this day, competition being very high on the stage lines between Sacramento and Stockton, they took advantage and $5 fared them both there.

Charlie, it is now September 2nd and I hear the Atlantic mail will be here on Monday for we most always hear of it or from it several days in advance. Therefore, I shall postpone further the above subject till next epistle.

September 4th. The day has arrived, Charlie, and also the mail and Snow is edified. Four letters came for Snow this mail and short but good was one from Little Fitz dated July 31st. I also received one from Cobb, which was *him* all over. I am now acting on the defensive, i.e., answering only letters received, NOT risking my chances voluntarily. Am glad the specimens went direct for the Post Master at Sonora said it was rather a suspicious package in looks for Uncle Sam's boys to handle, though the value of the specimens is not what I am thinking about, but the honesty of his clerks . . . . .

The morning you referred to, I believe I have some faint recollection and also the *letter.* The letter, if I mistake not, was very personal and reflected somewhat upon my character! However, the source from which it came was of so little consequence—to the man in the Moon—that Snow never returned to Bridgewater! Some say he went not from choice, others on the account of health, but more probably by acting in harmony with the wish of the faculty. But, as you say, it is "sad to think of these days," so you will allow me to pass.

I have laughed most heartily at your proposition of going West. The idea of coming home and going West when I am as far West as a Yankee can get, is a ludicrous one! But your meaning, I take, and if you will wait till I arrive, I will with pleasure accompany you. I am rather inclined to think that I have been a little nearer the setting sun than Fitz will ever get, though I hope not. For as the sun is elevated to appearances, you do not know what a beautiful prospect you have as the nearer you get. May you climb! In one of your epistles you seem quite exultant over the idea of you "Down Easters"—for all New England boys are called "Down Easters" here—seeing the sun some four hours before we do. But your feather is not very tall, for we never have to pry up Old Sol with a crow bar or wheel sunshine in a cellar to keep the potatoes from freezing and when any railroad accident happens, or steamboat disaster takes place, we have almost four hours to profit by your mishaps, guard against the evil, and examine the books.

You have probably noticed a *calm* in my correspondence for a few mails back, but such mail for the future will show that the air has been rarified. I have in my possession six letters from you. Please state in your next the number from me up to the first of August. Charlie, don't think me impudent, or not grateful, in my last by laying down a course for you to pursue in regard to writing or requiring you to write so often, for I merely said it that you might know what would be satisfactory to me.

Remember me to your parents, as far as proximity will permit. Do you correspond with P. now? If so, my respects. With lots of things that I have forgotten, I remain

Your friend,
Horace

May you become a Solomon in wisdom and an Astor in riches.

LETTER 9

Things Are Looking Up

Agua Frio, September 16th, 1854

Dear Charlie:

Seated on my three-legged stool before the old rustic table, I am happy to have health, materials, time and a mind to give you a few more details of my experience in California. But just let me give you a synopsis of a fortnight's change in our affairs. Since writing last an addition has been made to our family, or cabin, by one Spear, who accompanied your correspondent to this land of chances. He is now incorporated into and become one of us, striving after the same *needful*. We intend to remain in this very old cabin together till the time comes to throw down the shovel and the hoe and start for America. May it soon draw near? It almost seems like being back home again to be with Spear. We can talk about Boston, West Newton, Bridge-water, and many other things, and places, and really be there. At any rate, there in spirit, if not in body. One old friend and acquaintance is everything to a person's happiness in a distant land.

We are now laying in our winter's provisions and getting up our winter's wood. We can purchase provisions cheaper now than any other time and also cheaper by the quantity. In doing this, we capture two birds and come a "Yankee game," as the Southerners say. Twenty dollars is worth saving if your relatives are well off!—say two thousand miles off! I will tell you our kinds with prices and quantity annexed, just for a novelty. 50 lbs. butter @ .40; 2 bbls. flour @ $18.00; 1 bbl. crackers @ $10.00; 50 lbs. sugar @ .20; 12 lbs. chocolate @.36; 1

doz. boxes yeast powder $5.00; 15 lbs. candles @ .40; 30 lbs. lard @ .20; 50 lbs. of beans @ .10; and about $20.00 for extras, making a little bill of $122.00. This we calculate will last us till sunny spring begins to dawn and then we hope our pockets will look agreeable. These provisions are 30 percent cheaper

SINCE 1849, MARIPOSA TOWN HAS GROWN FROM A FEW TENTS TO A ROUGH LITTLE TOWN THAT CAN SUPPLY ALMOST ANYTHING!

now than a year ago the same time. The day is not far distant when necessaries of life will be nearly in line with Atlantic prices. A Pacific Rail Road is all we want. When that is built Snow is coming home! I suppose we shall have to look to the Know-Nothing Party for this accomplishment, as they seem to be one that "Does Something." They are spreading very fast in this country and wherever they have appeared, their ticket has been elected. We have three Know Nothings in our cabin—or I would say two—one by membership—Spear—and one by nature—Snow.

But to our wood pile, which I was going to pass. We have six cords of good nice oak wood piled or corded up in front of our cabin for winter use, an instance seldom found in California. We cut the wood about sixty rods from the cabin and with ourselves as the motive power, with a wheel barrow conveyed the same to the cabin. By each one's taking his turn, we kept the wheel moving and the pile growing. This winter when the winds howl and rains descend in torrents, when mud is feet deep and everything looks desolate, how happy Snow and his companions will be, snugly encased in the well-mossed cabin before a large fire of burning coals, reading the last Travellers from Little Fitz and recalling to memory times past gone. Give me the "latest news" and I am happy. But methinks you would like to know how I came to Agua Frio, as my last epistle left me in Stockton with funds beautifully reduced.

SIX CORDS OF WOOD WERE CONVEYED BY WHEELBARROW.

As we arrived in Stockton about nine in the evening, our first business was to obtain lodging for the night, which we accomplished for the sum of .75, having beat the man down .25 on a truthful pretext of poverty. But our lodging proved a dear one, if we estimate the price by the rest received, for we slept on barrel staves with scanty blankets and well filled with athletic and courageous and determined fleas, disagreeable companions in a restless night. Spear declares he never experienced such a night in all his life. By the way, after engaging our lodgings we found that the inner man must be strengthened, however the pocket might object. Therefore, we thought that some cheap dish could be obtained and partly compromise between hunger and pocket, so we repaired to a restaurant and called for two plates of beans! This greasy, unpalatable dish being devoured, we appeared before the bar and enquire the bill! $1.50, Sir! We remonstrated and pleaded our meager funds for excuse, but 'twas no use. This was their price and furthermore, with a coolness which harmonized with our palate and pocket, we were told that we could have had the best the house afforded at the same price! We left—not expelled—anyway, but good natured. At the first peep of day, Snow and Spear were in the streets—not with sore limbs and lacerated flesh! OH! No? Ready to embrace the first opportunity of gain and lay the foundation of our piles in California. As "Opposition is the life of business" we found the climate much excited and men waxing wroth at each other because of one's success in disposing of a ticket to a defunct merchant or strapped miner, for the Interior, and as we cared not whither we went, the whirlpool of contention soon brought us in to a vacuum and a maelstrom sacrifice tempted us to embark for Sonora. But our embarkation was not attended without "negotiations," for as we were without funds a verbal contract had to be drawn up stating that we should at some future time pay in the agent's hands in Sonora the sum of $8.00. This we willingly agreed to do as a matter of course and began to speculate upon our "manifest destiny," as Sonora was seventy miles into the Interior and we knew nothing of the place, not even by reputation. After our passage was secured to Sonora, we resolved—out of respect for the pocket—to commence the art of living without eating—a practice which we wish we had accustomed ourselves to before leaving America—as it costs a heap of money and never seems to satisfy. Therefore, without a breakfast and only $1.75 in our pockets, we took the stage and started for Sonora. Our conversation and feelings you can imagine during the day better than I can describe. However, we enjoyed the ride very much as our company was very jovial. Now Snow and Spear had been in the country long enough to get a few scales from off their eyes and understand the ropes considerable well, consequently they foresaw that it was the policy for the Stage Company to get possession of baggage for security should passengers be carried not exactly on the square. Therefore, they laid in with a brother tourist! to take unto himself the most valuable part of the aforesaid baggage that we might go on our way rejoicing in case the Agent should as contemplated. True to self interest and nature, no sooner were we before the office in Sonora than who should be accosted but Snow and Spear and politely requested to bring their baggage into the office. Of course, we had no objection to this and with a concaved valise walked in.

WE WENT TO SONORA, 70 MILES INTO THE INTERIOR.

Preliminaries being arranged, they took possession of the valise containing a half dozen old dirty shirts and their accompaniments and Snow and Spear began to search for something to eat, for it was now dark and their baked beans were among the things that were—and also for lodgings. Being a stranger in the place we thought best to enquire for a respectable boarding house and have some supper if were obliged to spend the last copper. Therefore, we were directed to the "Sierra Nevada" hotel and accordingly went and accordingly called for some supper! To suppose that we didn't eat our money's worth that night would be to suppose that all Normals keep the eight o'clock rule! Contrary to expectations we were allowed to retire without a word being said respecting pay. A rare instance in California.

Morning came and with it two strapped Yankees, strapped in pocket but not in spirits. Now, as Snow was a worker of wood, he resolved to leave not a stone unturned till he obtained work and in order to do this he went to the extreme lower end of Main Street and commenced asking every carpenter, right and left, as he returned back, but as fortune would have it, or something else, the fourth man enquired of gave him employment. The bargain was that Snow should commence after dinner and be supplied with tools and for his labor thereof receive $4.00 per day. With a light foot and also pocket, Snow found Spear and related his success, which once more inspired them with new courage and "press on" was their new motto. Snow went to work in the afternoon and remained with the same man six weeks. The first week his wages amounted to $18.00, which liquidated the stage debt and paid his board, $10.00. During the week his friend obtained the situation as steward or waiter in the "Sierra Nevada" and things began immediately to assume a different aspect. Instead of patronizing free lunches and compromising meals, I had my three good hearty set-downs every day, a good bunk to repose on, a few dimes to jingle in my pocket and prospects "which drove dull care away." The third week my wages were raised a dollar per day and easier work assigned me. But like all things in California, my job soon failed and I was again adrift upon a sea which swarmed with sharks and soulless bipeds.

It is now late and I must retire. We have just obtained an Atlantic paper and expect early next week an Atlantic mail. Therefore, I shall defer till then. Adios.

September 24th.

Charlie: The mail has now arrived and as could be expected, nothing for Snow. I have waited till the last moment for the mail and in consequence thereof am obliged to close. I intended to write two more pages but the next time will "bring up." The boys all send their best respects. Take mine and consider me your true chum. Write, if all you say is "From Little Fitz."

Horace.

[58]

LETTER 10

Yesterday, Today And Tomorrow

Agua Frio, October 4, 1854

Dear Charlie:

Today while diligently at work using the pick and shovel with credit meditating upon the riches which I shall soon possess? What should there come unto me but an epistle from Jennie, and strange to relate acting as companuerino—more probably as gallant—there came one from Little Fitz. Of course, I was a little pleased to see two old friends arm in arm

HORACE SNOW'S WARDROBE
...MUCH THE WORSE FOR
WEAR.

appear before me. Not being prepared for company, as my pants were in my boots and supported around my body by a leather strap being patched several times. Boots and hat decidedly the worse for wear and a woolen shirt which speaks for itself. Thus I was when you made your appearance but after sitting down and learning all I possibly could from you, I put you both in my pocket together and got excused till after ten in the evening. It appeared from Jennie that you paid her the very best attention during the voyage and was all to her that she could wish. No doubt you improved the opportunity and ascertained how James stood! Was very sorry that you received no letter the mail before writing for there was one due you of six pages. I have written you every mail since the middle of July and directed them all to West Newton. You must have written under poor encouragement not having received a letter from me for two mails. True, the blame upon Uncle Sam is OK. Your papers did not arrive in season last mail for acknowledgment but now we are once more thankful for your kindness. Our letters always arrive one mail in advance of papers. Your Normal news was very interesting. It seems as though I was there enjoying the company of all you spoke of. How well I shall be informed of the transactions when I return by your correspondence. And how much I shall be indebted to you for your trouble and expense. I hope some time I shall be able to make part amends. Would that I could be with you the day you penned your last letter September 1st. Say up in your room, with the elements giving down, talking over our actions since the first introduction since we were model scholars! I rather think the word model would have to be clipped from my name. That is if title expresses truth. We probably should not say much about posting ledgers or balancing accounts but Bridgewater scenes would have a thorough rehearsing. It seems to me that the Normal School, from what I can learn, is rather retrograding? I chose this inference from the small number attending. I can't think the present faculty equal in any respect to the former. I was not aware that Jairus Lincoln was sufficiently educated to be a competent teacher in that school. However, if all entries were as Snow was, but little education would be required to instruct him. Potter, it seems, is determined to accumulate more knowledge. I wonder what profession he intends following. By the way, I wrote him a long time ago and received no answer. Do you know whether he received

[60]

one from Me? How did Fletcher carry his head after gradu-ating? How well I remember the night we first landed in Boston . . . remember of riding up to our boarding house in a coach and also riding with a middle-aged man having a shaker pail full of domestic articles. I hardly thought such an old person as he would become a member of the Honorable 39th and how well I remember that gentle tap at the door, the cause of which went to present our majesties some refreshments and the duty of returning thanks devolving upon Snow. Do you remember the sardine supper? How I would like to meet about four of those girls . . . say the daguerrotype ones along with Little Fitz! If my calculations prove any way true, or near the truth, you and I will visit more than one of them and that too before one year has expired.

CHARLIE WILL
NOT KNOW ME . . .
AS I HAVE NOT
SHAVED . . . I LOOK
SOME PUNKINS!

J. BEARD

I am intending to visit America some time next year, that is, if my claims prove as good as I expect or even one half of it. Every morning we go to work we think of America and cal-culate how many miles this day's work will bring us there. Won't it be a glorious day with me when I land in Boston? Shall be so tickled that I shan't know how to act. If I have planned one arrival in Boston, I have five hundred and twenty-five! If Little Fitz is at the Traveller Office, I shall go there directly and take him by surprise, for he surely will not know me as I have not shaved since I left Boston. And then I shall go and buy me a stick of molasses candy. Yes, Charlie, I have not shaved me in the country and when I read your remarks upon Sanford Plympton, I thought you killed a bird which you little dreampt of. My whiskers are about four inches long, having been trimmed several times and moustache about three, all of a bright sorrel color and moustache parting directly in the middle of the olfactory organ and gracefully curling each way. I tell you I look some punkins! Whether I shall wear them back to America or not, I have not fully decided. Which way would you like to see me best?

October 7th.

Since commencing this epistle we have been reminded of approaching winter in the form of a gentle shower. This has not happened since the first of June. What an appearance would America present if no rain should fall for four months. See by the papers that it is very dry in the States and, by the way, your papers have come to hand, for which we are most thankful. Particularly Mr. Spear, for I never have seen a person so delighted with a speech or oration as he is with Mr. Peters. I think I never read anything better in my life. This is just such reading as we like to receive. Keep an account of your expenses and you shall be made whole.

Charlie, my prospects never were better in this world. I labor with a reasonable anticipation of possessing next spring a pretty little sum. I mean a pretty sum for a young man unencumbered with a family and wishing to settle down and commencing some business. We have just laid out $300 and with our work, expect to realize a profit of $3,000 next spring, but, after all, luck may be against us. Mining is in one sense all luck. Today your claim may pay abundant and tomorrow be worthless. The mining in this county is very spotty. That is the gold is not distributed evenly over the diggings but lies in deposits. To show you, there was a hole sunk in a claim that we worked out last winter. In '49 $3,000 was taken out. Nothing else could be found around it. Had they not been lucky and sunk exactly over the gold, perhaps your friend would have been more flush now. Last winter our division was too large and I learned that the larger the division, the smaller the dividends. Eight was the pretty little number that divided each day's work the greater part of last winter. The cause of this was my working upon shares. This year I am my own man, own my "Tom," shovels, hose and claims. Though to enlarge our business we have bought in with another man. 2, 3 and 4 will be the division this winter. Should I visit America next spring, I shall do it with the intention of returning to the El Dorado again.

TOO MANY PARTNERS.

I just learned by the papers that a new mail or steamboat arrangement has gone into operation whereby the price of passage is fixed permanent for one year and that to be very high. This may have something to do with my coming home. I shall hardly be willing to pay $300 for a ticket to New York. Spear and I have always talked of taking passage in a clipper ship when we return and go by the way of China, England, etc. And this steamboat cost may make a reality of it. If we should do so, we should not arrive in Boston till late in the Fall. However, I am undecided about anything. Next May will solve all of these difficulties. May, May and a yellow pocket. . . .

This is Saturday afternoon and a half day set aside to do our washing and such like things. The boys are out hunting quail and by the reports, I expect we shall have a quail pie for dinner tomorrow. Please call in and dine with us. Warrant all dishes palatable.

THE CALIFORNIA QUAIL. A WELCOME CHANGE FROM BEANS.

Charlie, I hardly know what I would do were I in your place respecting teaching and leading a mercantile life. Had I the foundation and taste for a scholar as you have, I might be induced to prepare for a literary profession but, as I know my tastes are decidedly mercantile, I think a person selecting an occupation or business for life should consult their constituents and their health, for good health is the great secret of all success. Now, if a sedentary life has a bad effect upon your health, destroying your vital energy, I should certainly say lead a mercantile life. A mercantile life is unquestionably the most lucrative, though the first few years seem like uphill business. But one thing certain, I would follow no business or remain in any employment where it was injuring my health. As the darkest hour is just before day, something soon will turn up for your advantage. In the meantime, drink lots of new milk and grow. Should I return next summer and all things being favorable, we will take a trip out West sure. Save your coppers for one hundred make a dollar . . . Spear sends his best regards. Next mail you can expect another. From your short lived chum, and roommate and friend,

Horace.

LETTER 11

The Bread That Flopped

Agua Frio, California
October 9, 1854

Dear Charlie:

I am in great trouble! Troubled exceedingly in my domestic affairs. Good bread being an indispensable article in promoting health and happiness, I am sorry to say we have not got. But the trouble lies with the yeast. Whether by accident or neglect or whether by carelessness or some other misdemeanor, I know not, but somehow or other we are out of yeast. Twice have we made trial according to directions and twice have we failed. For two long days has our last batch been exposed to the sun and for twice many long nights has the homogenous mass occupied a space on the warm hearth but, in spite of our ill looks, our indignant rhetoric, and all violation of chemical laws, this aforesaid compound is just as sweet as the moment we had it prepared. We begin to think that each ingredient belongs to the peace society and consequently the greatest of harmony prevails. Now, if we could only instigate one part or portion to rise up in rebellion against the rest, or pick a bit of a fuss with its neighbor, then our aim would be accomplished. But such a thing seems almost impossible. What action we shall take in the premises, I am not prepared to say at this moment but something desperate will be done soon. Next mail you shall hear the particulars.

Your letter of September 1st has come to hand and it is truly a welcome messenger. It was the only letter that I received but made up for a large number. I am glad that my dilatory epistles have caught up so that you may know where the blame is. Your epistle has come too late for me to answer those questions but next mail I will try and give you as good a description as I can. I usually commence my letters and get them nearly done before the mail arrives, but this time I have been so busy. Remember the yeast that I have deferred till now? I have not been very well

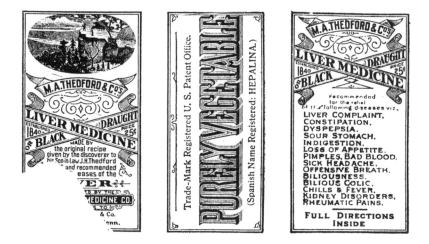

for the last weeks owing, I think to irregular bathing, but now I am convalescent. We are still throwing up dirt, which operation I will better explain you next time, and making other preparations for coming winter. Such things as fresh plastering the outside of the cabin; topping out the chimney; putting a fly over the roof; rearranging our bunks, etc. With our cabin well provisioned, with a good quantity of dirt ready for washing, with a good wood pile before our door, we wait patiently for "King storm not to stay his hand" . . . .

Evening of the 9th   The mail brought today, three Waverlys, one Traveller, and a Telegraph for which you cannot imagine the joy they gave us. Nothing does us so much good as a goodly number of papers. One good letter and a few papers just puts me on a pinnacle of human happiness. To be at work in the claim picking and shoveling and have a person bring me one or two letters, with a handful of papers and, seemingly, there is no bound to my strength or powers of endurance—created in an instance. Charlie, like all the blessings of life you have only to be deprived of them to know their worth. I haven't slept upon a common bedstead since the last night in New York and now, when I arise in the morning, instead of putting my lily-white feet upon a soft carpet or mat, I am obliged to place them upon the bare bosom of Mother Earth. The old lady's bosom gets pretty cold these nights by morning, but a few steps brings me to the warm fireplace and then all is right. Every night when we retire we hurry up some wood partly burnt so that in the morning we always have a splendid bed of coals to warm our toes by and build a fire upon.

Let me tell you of one day in our lives. Say the one just past. The morning I awoke very early and was thinking about—well, I have forgotten what—when all at once a big rat who was running along the logs missed his calculations and fell smack into my stationery box. This aroused me from my calm content and in less than one minute I was up, had a candle lit and after him with a sharp stick—for I always keep one beside me expressly for this purpose. I hunted him around the flour barrel, the dutch oven, the pile of wood, but at last he got away from me, "knowing better the ropes" and made good his escape. Not having violated the 13th Commandment, I now built a fire and began to prepare breakfast. I first put some water on to heat to wash the dishes with, for just as we were done with supper last night, our nearest neighbor made us a call and so we deferred till morning, though this was against one of our regulations. As soon as the water was hot, I put the chocolate on and washed the dishes. I had no need to cook this morning as we had beans yesterday and they were not all gone. Bread we always bake night beforehand. Therefore, before the first rays of sun peeped over the hills, I had breakfast all ready, which frugal meal consisted as follows: beans, boiled ham, bread, butter, cheese, chocolate, cold water, boiled rice, sugar, with pepper, vinegar and salt. And, true to say, I was the only person up to enjoy the warm breakfast and morning air. However, by relieving them of a few blankets, I soon had them before the fire! Breakfast being over, we put the unconsumed food in the cupboard, which, by the way, is a Natick shoe box,

turned our plates the other side up, changed our woolen shirts
and went to work, which time was about sun half hour high.
We picked and shovelled until noon—our guide being the
shade of a tree—when my brother brought a pail of water. I
built a fire, and Spear set the table. Dinner the same as breakfast, substituting tea for chocolate. Afternoon the same as
forenoon and when night came my brother made the bread,

BEST CABIN ON THE CREEK.

Spear washed the dishes and I boiled the rice. We had rice and
molasses for supper, with a sprinkling of biscuit and butter. As
we have no milk, we use molasses in its stead. The day passes in
this way and all for a *little Money!* Now, Charlie, I must be
excused from writing more. The boys are reading the papers
and keep continually talking to me. It is "Just hear this,
Horace," "Hold on one moment," "Hurrah for America,"
"Three cheers for Old Boston," and so on. Now add this to my
eagerness to get hold of the papers and you must know that my
rudder is unshipped. It is all my fault and the like shall never
happen again. The boys offer more regards than I can enclose
and wish you the *Prince of Greatness.* More next time certain.

Yours truly in haste,
from chum, Horace.

N.B. Send us a "Know Nothing" for we would have one in our
cabin by invitation.

[68]

LETTER 12

Gold Pans In Competition

Agua Frio, California, (Of course)
Oct. 22nd, 1854

Dear Charlie:

Last Wednesday—Oct. 18th—I was favored with another long and interesting epistle from you. It came the quickest of any letter ever received, only 23 days to Frisco. Why my letters fail reaching you in proper season is more than I can understand. I have not put a letter in the Post office since I returned from Sonora but what I have enquired of the Post Master whether I was in season or not and have always been answered in the affirmative. If the middle of August mail from California had arrived when you dated your letter, you should have received another one, for I have written you every mail since the middle of July. I hope by this time Uncle Sam has made you aware of Snow's thankfulness to his *true and never failing* correspondent. In several of my letters I have given you a meager description of my first proceedings in California. Whether it will be interesting to you or not a few months will tell, but I hope as a whole be acceptable. In one of my letters— forget which one—I enclosed a two and half dollar piece which I hope by this time you are in possession of. Should this go direct, I shall venture more. I occasionally send you an engraving representing some California scene. But one of these days I am going to send *Myself* and you may rest assured that there will be no delay. About next 4th of July I reckon we will talk about "Auld Lang Syne." I am determined to visit America next summer, if possible. I want to get back there once more, have a good time, see different parts of the country, and then I shall be content to leave for a long period. I have acquired a great disposition to travel within twenty years and my curiosity will not be satisfied till I have visited many parts of the Old World. Being single and no trouble of housekeeping, I intend a few of my years shall be spent in a way which can be looked back to as pleasant and interesting. What pleasure it must give a person to say and think that once he has gazed at ruins and works of art erected thousands of years ago, that he has travelled over the same ground as the patriarchs of old, that he has stood before those huge monuments upon the bank of the Nile where the "oldest inhabitants" know not the beginning of! Yes, Charlie, I must see them, but enough of this, for I hear you say he had better go to School a few more months and then be better prepared to understand these things when they are seen. You say you have some idea of going to your Uncle's next Spring and spending the Summer, this in preference to all other plans. I sincerely hope you will do so. No matter about literary fame in juvenile years, no matter about developing the mind to its fullest extent before the physical organization is quite perfect. Let them keep pace together. Let a foundation for a good healthy physical structure be laid and then all other things can be added. Better be healthy and letterless at twenty-one than able to translate Virgil with an undermined constitution. You want the country air. You want to let Books alone for a season and invigorate and strengthen your system. I judge from your letters that your health is not first rate, and the more you keep confined and the closer you apply yourself to books— at the present time—the less happiness you are going to enjoy hereafter. I believe there is a chance for you to grow some more and nothing but driving the cows to pasture and drinking new milk will do! I must confess that I am a little selfish in this, for if you go into the country next Spring, I can have a much better time with you when I return. I anticipate some pleasant rambles with you next Summer. However, I think you will never regret next summer spent in this way. The idea is you must *grow* to be a man! I think you are enjoying yourself pretty well these times going round to see the girls, going to conventions, corresponding, making love, etc.

How happy a person can be if he has plenty of acquaintances—ladies preponderating—and plenty of money! He can bask in the sunshine, drink lemonade and go where he pleases.

Your invitation to accompany you to Salem I think I must decline, for I have not a very particular regard for Mr. Boyden and think I will never trouble his attention again. However, I think he did nothing but what he thought was his duty. Most any other place I would have been with you. There are about twenty places in the New England States that I shall visit if ever I return again, that is with a *Yellow* Pocket.

Our White Mountain tour will come off then. How we will eat plums and milk while travelling. We shall have to visit Provincetown, Nantucket, Newport and all round Cape Cod. But there is no use in talking, there is too many a "slip between the cup and the lip." I may be obliged to remain over another year.

It seems that Smith has written me several times, but only one epistle has come to hand. I presume the number can be resolved into two in *one*, for letters come very direct now. Every pamphlet and paper spoken of in your letters has arrived and all been acknowledged. Your last Traveller was the best one I have received. Mr. Sumner's speech was capital. I love to read

ABOLITIONIST SNOW FEARS CALIFORNIA WILL BECOME A SLAVE STATE.

his speeches. There is no such thing as "True Democracy" in California. Slavery has a strong hold here. I hear it said that three-fourths of all the officers in this State are Southern men. How much do you think of your lucky classmates in the "Hon. 39th"? I wish I could remember how often I think of them. We seemed to belong to that class only in rotation. Please write me how your class came out in spelling the second term. I think Mr. T. encouraged them a little at the "change of books."

Then Stephens has taken his summer tour to the fashionable and been up to Champlain! Now I have a Brother that used to visit the White Mountains every few years, but always forgot to say that he had been home to see his Father! Perhaps Stephens forgets to say that he was born on the York side of Lake Champlain.

No "facsimile." I think I will bring myself next summer, as you will be more sure of getting it, but should I not come, I shall trust it to Uncle Sam. I will be an awful looking thing!

Where is Wight? I believe I must write him, as I never have. Please inform me of his whereabouts. I think times must be very dull in West Newton, the Normal School being gone and no capitalists investing anything there. Though I suppose Mr. Allen's school makes up in part for the Normal. Am glad to hear that he is doing so well.

We are still at the same employment. Everything goes right. All healthy, contented and satisfied. We have showers now very often and expect winter very soon. Our choice would be to have rain the 1st of December, but it may come sooner or may later. The rains held off last year till the first of January. In "50" they had no rain at all. If this year should prove so "chum Snow" would be *down*. Last week our company, consisting of four,

THROWING UP DIRT.

stripped off four feet from a pit sixty feet long and nine feet wide and threw up the bottom of a foot and a half more. We throw off the top dirt, level it smooth, and throw up the bottom, which prepares it nice for winter. There are but few men, Charlie, that can handle the pick and shovel as dexterious as Snow!

We have had another "Steamboat disaster" on this side in which the Yankee Blade and some 30 or so passengers are no more. It does seem strange that the Pacific Ocean is not wide enough for steamers to ply between San Francisco and Panama. Nearly every disaster on this side has been caused by hugging the shore so closely to save distance that they have run

ANOTHER "STEAMBOAT DISASTER."

into rocks. What is one day's more sail to the hazard of eight hundred lives? I know a little something of a "Shipwreck" by experience. How much I shall have to talk about when I get home. I believe I could interest you for six months and then be quite fertile. If I only had concentration to bring it together and present it in some form, I would like it very much. My task in writing would half be diminished. I suppose you will allow me to change my subjects as often as Past Masters do their politics, therefore, I'll tell you this.

Last summer while my brother and I were throwing up alone, there was quite a competition to see who would wash out the best pan—the one containing the most gold. To have the affair go straight, we agreed that we should take turns in washing, first my brother, then myself and so on. When we got down to the ledge the one in turn would pick his place, scrape up a pan full and go and wash it. Things went on in this way till the 12th day of August without much difference, the biggest pan being $5.00—I believe which I wrote you—which was washed up by Calm Snow. This day when we came to the ledge my brother began to pick around—it being his turn—and accidently struck a place which looked nearly yellow with gold!! He jumped for the pan and began to fill it and I looked on. I saw by the dirt that he would take the palm from my honored head and began to remonstrate against his selecting the dirt in such a way and also for rounding up his pan so. But this was no use! Finally, I offered him a *dollar* to let me wash the pan. But this was no use! He was bound to wash the pan and away he went. He returned in a few moments and how much do you guess he obtained. Only $19.75! Now chum Snow wasn't idle by no means while he was gone and accidentally discovered him a place but when he saw his brother's gold he thought 'twas no use, for $19.75 was a tremendous pan.

THE PRICE OF GOLD IN 1854 WAS
$17.00 PER OUNCE.

HORACE AND
BROTHER HIT A
LUCKY POCKET.

However, Snow kept on picking and in a short time got him a pan. Our competition had become very great, so much so, that my Brother had to go and see me wash it, for fear that I should come some game upon him. The pan when washed, the gold dried and weighed and, Charlie, how much do you reckon I had? Only the pitiable sum of $48.50!! Wasn't I tickled! Just think how exciting it must be to take a common tin pan such as dairy women use for milk and fill it full of dirt and wash out $48.50 in it? We washed out another pan and obtained $23.75, making in all $92.00 in three pans, and in one day! The rest we threw up not caring for the scattered lumps. Such little things like these make the days and weeks pass very pleasantly. But this is no criterion to judge our claim by. Next winter will only tell. Charlie, you cannot think how well we are situated. We have the best Cabin, the best table, the best bunks, the best dishes, the most books and more conveniences than any other cabin in Agua Frio Camp. Sometimes I think that I could spend my days here, only give me plenty of papers and enough to read.

Helen says she can't believe that I am going to be an Old Bachelor, when one has been so frank, etc., but such things in the wisdom of Nature will happen. Helen wrote me a splendid letter. Please remember me to her.

Charlie, this letter will be put in the Post office the 23rd of this month to be in season for the mail the 1st of November. The mails on this side leave the 1st and middle of every month. May this reach you one month from date. Fearing your patience will not hold out with my subject, I close, hoping, wishing, and remaining as ever, your true chum, friend and classmate,

Horace C. Snow

More next mail.

LETTER 13

Justice In Mariposa

Agua Frio, Cal.
December 4th, 1854

Dear Charlie:

Yesterday, agreeable to expectations, I received another interesting epistle from you bearing date Nov. 3rd. We heard of the arrival of the mail in Frisco four days previous to their

WORDS FROM HOME ARE WORTH A 'YELLOW POCKET.'

appearance here, a piece of intelligence which generally has some trouble with patience. Your letter came singly forth this time and consequently was read and re-read till nearly committed to memory.

Would that you could see the smile of joy that lights up

Snow's brown and natural countenance when he receives from the Postmaster those sacred epistles. Who but an exile, or a Californian, knows the value of a letter? When the mail arrived yesterday—Sunday—there were some thirty or forty of us at the Postoffice waiting and when the mail was opened, we were all crowded up around the counter six or eight deep and the person that stood next to me was so excited that I could feel his heart beat against my side as plain as though my hand was upon it. He was fortunate to receive a letter, it being the second one after almost four years absence. Every letter written in California I have set down in a book and when the answer comes I make an X and this X will be the criterion which I shall judge my friends by. There will be a good many *supposed* friends found wanting. You think in your letter that I am well "located as regards domestic affairs." etc. I am sorry to say that you have rather a wrong impression. Not very wrong but more disagreeable. Just imagine yourself in a log cabin with several other persons and taking your turn in getting up in the morning and building the fire and getting the breakfast. Tomorrow morning you are to get up. You wish to be up early because the other boys did so and you don't wish to be laughed at. You retire early; the last thought which lingers on the brain being "I'll beat Spear if I can" . . . Morning begins to dawn and agreeable to the last thought, you are awake. You rub your eyes and look for daybreak, but the cracks in the cabin are not discernable, consequently, you know not the hour of the night. You fall into a dreamy mood and think of sirloin steak, plum puddings, mince pies, potted pigeons, warm rooms, carpeted floors, convenient stoves, fresh papers, etc. etc., and never once imagine that you will awake to disappointment. But ah! it comes, and with it discernable openings in the Old Log Cabin! Now you know it is time to turn out! But where will you find courage for such a dangerous enterprise? Here you are, perched upon two poles five feet from the ground; no chair to step into, no mat to jump onto; but a few pegs in a post to assist you in ascending and descending. Every move must be done with caution, for the least mistake might peril a limb and perhaps life. Slowly and cautiously you creep your way down—to the last peg, where you make a halt. Before retiring and knowing well what had to come, you place your old shoes at the foot of the ladder and also the stockings. Here, with one hand-hold of the post, you manage with the other to dress your feet; jump into the old shoes and launch forth onto the uncarpeted and unfloored bottom of the Old Cabin. NB. As you are up now I think I will retire, so good night.

6th. Well, Charlie, I intended to have written you some more last night but Spear was fortunate enough to receive four papers after supper and I was obliged to peruse them. Your papers have not arrived. Rather curious that Spears should come and mine not, both from and to the same place. Well, to resume the above, or rather, to close, for you are rather *kept in the dark*. I would say that the hardest part is over with—unless the teapot should tip over and put the fire all out—for you take much consolation in thinking that if all housekeepers are as much troubled with each dish as you are with ham and beans, that you, alone, are not the only sufferer. But after all, "the miner's life is the life for me—I own I love it dearly."

Charlie, today I have been *a-courting*! True, Sir—This morning I fixed up in my best bib and tucker and by invitation went to Mariposa. I was cordially received and enjoyed myself to the utmost all day. I have another invitation to call again tomorrow and think I shall go. How pleasant it is after many months' denial to meet with a company of Ladies and Gentlemen and spend a few hours in social conversation. Yes, I hear you say, it must be, but the great trouble in this case, was that there were no Ladies! Yesterday, while picking away in my claim, a gentleman appeared before me and says, "Your name, Sir?" "What?", says I. "Please give me your name?" By this time, I knew what was up and says my name is Snow. "Your first name, if you please," says he, "and be quick, for the other boys are all *running* and I want to catch them." "Horace C. Snow, sir," says I. Then says he, "Mr. Snow, I warn you to appear at Mariposa tomorrow morning at ten o'clock to serve as a *Grand Jurorman*, whereof fail not or suffer the penalty of

PROSPECTIVE
JURORS EAGER TO
SERVE!

the law."—and away he ran to catch some of the other boys who had, unintentionally, of course, gone in search of something. The boys were too sharp for him and he only got *two* out of *seven*. Miners, as a general thing, are much averse to sitting upon a jury. They get no pay, (not enough to bear expenses), besides losing their time and disarranging their work. You would laugh to see the miners take to the bushes when the Sheriff makes his appearance on the creek. Well, we appeared before *His Honor*, took the prescribed oath, organized and proceeded to business. Up to our adjournment tonight, we found five bills. I have walked ten miles today and feel fatigued, therefore, Adios.

December 9th. Well, Charlie, I resume my pen again to say a few words more before the 10th arrives. I am now a common plain citizen, having discharged my duty as becomes a scholar, gentleman, and patriot. I sat two days as an honorable Grand Juror of Mariposa County, California! Never, Sir, in the history of my life have I been so honored, have I been placed in such a responsible situation, have I been placed where an uprightness of character and sense of understanding was so essential and finally, never have I been so thoroughly tried in the scale of public opinion as now! You have only to know a person's character to appreciate it! True greatness will work its way out. Tell all the Doctor O___s and Professor Boydens that

MARIPOSA CHRONICLE:

W. T. WHITACRE & A. S. GOULD,
PROPRIETORS AND PUBLISHERS.

FRIDAY, FEBRUARY 3, 1854

At present, our courts are generally held in small and confined rooms, where there is scarcely space enough for the Court and Bar, not to speak of the Juries. We have now a very good and secure jail, which has already saved the county more than the cost of building, in the way of guards for the prisoners, besides being infinitely more secure. Now as to economy, we understand that the County pays about three hundred dollars per month for rent of public offices; these we are compelled to have, as she law directs it, and public convenience demands it. And in addition thereto, at every term of a Court almost, a room or two has to be rented for the use of the Grand Jury ; the Trial Juries being compelled to come to "sage conclusions," the foreman either on a rock, or stump, and the other jurors surrounding him as old Virgil says, "under the *patulating* shade of an *umbragous fag* tree." (See_ 1st Georgics en passant.)

Now would it not be better to erect a suitable building, sufficiently large for a Court House, and rooms for the juries and public officers? This certainly could be done if properly managed at a comparatively small cost, lumber selling now at very low rates.

This is a matter which calls for immediate attention, and we hope that the Honorable Court of Sessions will not consider us arrogant in thus calling their attention to the matter.

THE CHRONICLE CALLS FOR A COURTHOUSE! A CONTRACT FOR A $9000 BUILDING WAS SIGNED ON JUNE 1, 1854. HORACE WAS SUMMONED FOR JURY DUTY TWICE BEFORE THE COURTHOUSE WAS FINISHED. HE MUST HAVE SEEN IT DURING CONSTRUCTION BUT LEFT MARIPOSA BEFORE IT WAS OFFICIALLY OPEN FOR BUSINESS.

the sturdy oak my bend to the storms and its branches give way to the sweeping blasts, but when the morrow comes it is sure to right itself again. Who knows what my future may be? Who knows but what future generations may sing praises to my honor! Nobody, Sir!! *Maximus in Minimus!* Now, Charlie, don't think from the above that I am forgetting my origins or that I feel *above* you, for such is not the case. However I may be exalted, publicly or privately, I shall look upon you as the same "Little Fitz" and Dear friend. Though our stations in after-life may be far apart, yet I shall always extend the same hand of fellowship as in days of adversity.

[81]

Your papers have just arrived tonight, Charlie. I have not read them yet but just glanced over them. Thank you again! Next mail will send you a gold dollar. Mr. Spear has been grinding over some old poetry for your benefit—and produced the enclosed. You will not prize it for the poetry but the feeling or intention. I would like to answer many points in your letter but have not time. I work very hard day times and when I get our cooking done in the evenings I feel very much like climbing up onto those two poles and staying there till morning. I never saw the need of the other "two fourth" till I came here. Don't wonder the young men are all getting married in America. Your wish seems to be very moderate. "A retired farm, plenty of literature, friends, good health, and somebody to view the heavens with and be happy!" How easy this can be obtained! Seemingly you have but "to propose," make a purchase and you are the happiest man in the world! May your *modest wish* be realized. I can think of nothing but a splendid mansion, beautiful walks, sparkling fountains, refreshing shades, costly carriages, numerous servants, and some beautiful "Countess" for a Mrs. Snow! What a difference in our aim! My mark is high but I think my present course and success forebodes the achievement of it. I shall then—as a matter of course—give dinners of State to which you may expect invitation!!

We have had cloudy weather for some weeks now and considerable rain, but not enough for mining purposes upon our creek. Everybody expects right smart rain very soon. When I commenced this letter, I thought one sheet would be all I could possibly fill out, but abounding in shallow nonsense, you have this much more. Partners wish you prosperity and success. Give my uncultivated regards to Helen. I will do better next mail.

> From Horace, Just and True
> (Adios - Sp.)
> (Goodbye)

LETTER 14

Gold Dust And Liniment

Agua Frio, California
December 20th, 1854

Dear Charlie:

As negligence will happen in all families, you must expect that it will in mine occasionally. I have been trying for the last week to commence this epistle but honestly could find no convenient time till now. You probably think that I have these long evenings all to myself and wonder how I while away time and perhaps even wish you were as well situated, but a few things I will explain to you. In the first place, our kitchen, sleeping, dining and literary room is one and the same thing, being all upon the ground floor. Congregated in this cabin— or room—there is flour, crackers, pork, ham, beans, lard, rice, sugar, etc., besides, though not least, three *hombres*. Yes, there is more! There are pots, kettles, pans, stools, barrels, boxes, pails, wood, bunks, shelves, boots, clothing, pistols, hose, etc. Now, as all miners take the privilege of coming and going when they please, you must expect, now and then, to receive a call and especially where there are a good many to receive them pretty often, and, as a matter of consequence, to make a few yourself. Add to this the unusual attraction to our cabin caused by our *books, papers, knowledge,* and my old *Atlas,* and you will see that writing is sometimes out of the question. And still, where there are three persons in one room and two of them so full of patriotism and "76" that they can't read, write, or keep still and you are again in a bad fix; and furthermore, imagine the indifference caused by cramped fingers, swollen wrists, and painful shoulders and you have enough. Tonight an Irish neighbor said he should call but he has not arrived yet and the boys have gone over to the store, so I am all alone just as I

Young & Johnson,
MAIN STREET, AGUA FRIO,
General Dealers in Groceries and Provisions,
KEEP on hand a general assortment of Fresh and DESIRABLE GOODS, and at the most reasonable rates. Our stock is well assorted and we think with our prices, will give general satisfaction to those who may favor us with their patronage. feb3-tf

would like to be four evenings out of the seven. How much more I can read, study, meditate and improve my mind when alone. "O! for a lodge in some wilderness."

The 17th day of this month, Charlie, brought the great North American mail in to Agua Frio. Your letter of Nov. 12th was received, and also one from Cobb. The 19th brought papers and such a good time as we have had you certainly never experienced. I mean in a *periodical* point of view.

Your letter lies before me so interesting and so long that I dare not attempt a respectable answer this mail. For your kindness, trouble, patience and expense in furnishing me with so much news, mental and foreign, I am dumb. Thanks profit nothing. As you know something of my disposition and as "actions speak louder than words," this will be where my gratitude shall be manifested.

You wish to know very particularly *when* I shall *return*. I cannot give any decided answer as the time will depend upon the mining season and our *luck*. Bad luck—no *America!* Good luck, old New England and its comely girls! My last day of mining last spring was the 13th day of June and if this season should prove about the same as last, you might expect me in the "Athens of America" about the first of August and perhaps the middle of July, everything being favorable. Your correction about my being in "America" after all, Charlie, I think is not correct. If the peel of an orange is in the orange, then California is in America, but if the peel of the orange is not in the orange, then California is not in America. California no doubt belongs to America—however, a stranger might think China the best represented, especially geographically, but mentally, morally, and spiritually, she is decidedly foreign. *Incontrovertible logic!* That above! Like Smith, I must adhere to the first impression. Hark? I hear the boys coming! Therefore, I shall have to close till tomorrow evening.

December 21st, 1854. Another hard day has passed and with it has brought our throwing up dirt to a termination. We have labored for the last four months, most remarkably hard, not losing but one or two days excepting Saturday afternoon. I feel tonight—physically—just like a hard worked draft horse. My fingers are so stiff that I can hardly hold my pen; my arms and shoulders ache; my sides are lame and I am somewhat indisposed, but mentally, I feel just as well as I ever did. We are now going to recruit up before the rainy season sets in if we have time and according to present appearances, we shall have plenty for it looks not so much like rain now as it did a month ago. However, last year we had no rain of any account till after New Years. Everybody has predicted rain this change of the moon and many a glass of whiskey has gone where scores have gone before at the failure. Some say we are not going to have any rain this winter for the reason that the deer and elk are all going back into the mountains. I believe it is a fact that deer and such game generally winter on the plains just as fashionable merchants live "out of town" in the summer. There being no snow on the plains in the winter they fare much better. Whether instinct tells the deer right or not, a few months can only decide. I think they ought to know, for I believe they lived here before ever man did and what is more, they have nothing else to do but study the weather and get a living. And, by the way, we have the best venison to eat that ever was sold in the world! We can buy the very best saddles of venison for eighteen cents per pound. Good roast venison graces our table almost every day. Charlie, if you want to know how to relish a good meal of victuals, just come out to California and *cook it.* Do you think you and I would have prospered at Bridgewater if we had done our own cooking? I think that a gentle tap at our door such as the first one proved to be would be very acceptable. Mother's cakes and Aunt's pies would have been in good demand. But now, Charlie, our table would groan under the ponderous weight of its well-filled dishes.

I see you go down onto the sea shore quite often since graduating. May be that there is considerable attraction down there. Truly, that school seems to be losing popularity. I think the great epoch whereby to judge the beginning of the downfall was at my expulsion. Somehow or other I have but little sympathy for that school, although I think I was justly acted with. This is not so good a spirit, but I am too far away to cultivate a better one for the present. But when I return to *America* I'll not say aught against them.

What a pity it is for me that I am your senior by a few years! That the responsibility of introducing some subject for discussion rests upon me. Now you see, Charlie, I thought as you were quite young and had just left school, that I would let you choose some subject best suiting your tastes and inclinations as you might take more interest in the matter and, as a matter of course, it could not make any difference with me!! Now, Charlie, I have two other letters to write this mail and maybe I shall not get time to write you anymore; therefore, I hope you will excuse this meager sheet and give me an opportunity to redeem my pledges next mail. I enclose in this a gold dollar which I want you to appropriate in the following way: Purchase me a Boston Almanac, pay the postage, then take one half of the remainder, expend the same for stationery for your purposes, and with the rest spend it all for the next two succeeding mails for papers, reserving postage as a matter of course. When I write to you to keep an account of what monies you spent for me I didn't mean to have you keep an account of what monies I sent you, but what money you paid out of your pocket so that I might not be any expense to you. With the hope of writing some more before too late, I will close now in the same familiar manner.

Your true friend,
"Horace."

LETTER 15

Murders On Impulse

Cabin de Snow & Co.,
Agua Frio, Dec. 31, 1854

Dear Charlie:

Ever since last writing you has my brain been making furious revolves in seeking after some subject or topic wherein I might display that "oratorical" power of Demosthenes or philosophical genius of Franklin, but alas! I have found none. With my granite foundation Model contour and Normal finish I have most admirably succeeded in a beautiful failure. Every subject which presented itself to my mind having two sides was so quickly settled that I could hardly believe my own conclusions and furthermore, as I always took the right side and thought such powerful logic, I came to the sensible conclusion—suppose—that you would be immediately convinced and, consequently, no argument could be had. And, besides all this, there were two other things which materially helped me in coming to this supposed sensible conclusion; First, how in the name of Washington could you discuss some or any subject when hard study and deep thought were necessary for a brilliant production the day before the 4th of July or some other holiday?

On the same thing, supposing you possessed untold sums of gold and all that was necessary to place the shining ore before you was water, and the Heavens showed indications of supplying the liquid any day? What would be the state of your mind? Calm, sober and reflective, or would it be jolly, lively, sportive, etc? Secondly, and lastly, the superior abilities of my antagonist both natural and cultivated counsel me, "as discretion is the better part of valor"—to avoid any conflict as long as harmony could be preserved. However, as my brain is very fertile, something new may spring up before I get through.

MARIPOSA CHRONICLE:

WHITACRE & GOULD, EDITORS.

MARIPOSA:

FRIDAY, FEBRUARY 3, 1854

BEAR VALLEY.—The Mexicans and Chileans of Bear Valley have lately been trying their cutting and shooting powers to an unusual extent. It was but a few days since, that a Chilean, without the least provocation, made an attack on Mr. Wm. Hamilton, with a knife, and severely wounding him in the thigh. Mr. H. then drew his revolver and fired, but missed—the Mexican still following up the attack. Mr. H. then fired two more shots, both taking effect. The Chilean lived but a few minutes after.

On Sunday night last there was a row at the same place amongst the "greasers," in which there were three severely wounded,—one by a knife and two by pistol shots.

Now, let me speak a few words about town. One or two days after I closed my last letter to you, another *horrible murder* was committed within one half mile of our cabin. The murder was committed at a Mexican camp, one that has sprung up within a few months. The tragedy occurred at a gambling table, there being some trouble about the bets, a few words passed and one drew a bowie knife and stabbed the other in the mouth, severing the jugular vein, causing death in a few moments. The murderer made his escape, but not without getting wounded from several revolvers which were fired at him, as he was traced a long way from the blood which left him. This affair happened in the evening. This caused considerable excitement for a few days, but now is among the things that were. Murders are so common here that the people hardly enquire into them unless they happen to know one of the parties. There have been, to my knowledge since I came here, *TWELVE* murders within fifteen miles of this place. It is just so all over California. A short time ago three men up North started on a prospecting tour and had proceeded but a short distance when they were attacked by a band of fourteen robbers. The robbers rose up from behind some small bushes and fired at the miners, expecting to kill them at the first shot, but,

TWELVE MURDERS
WITHIN FIFTEEN
MILES OF OUR CABIN.

fortunately, they only killed one and in an instant the other two drew their revolvers and commenced returning the shots, but in a few moments only one miner was standing. He, with the most cool courage and deadly aim I ever heard of, shot ten of the robbers dead on the spot, having discharged every barrel of two revolvers. The other four being out of loads also made a rush at him with their bowie knives, confident of victory at last, I suppose, but they were mistaken. The miner proved too much for them and in a few moments two more were laid low, one mortally wounded—who has since died—and the other disabled and also marked for life, having lost his nose. The second miner, who was shot down, is now in a fair way of recovery. This miner who stood the fire had his clothes pierced by over thirty balls and yet he escaped with only two or three flesh wounds. One of the robbers made a confession before he died and stated that they were a regular, organized band and had killed Chinese, Mexicans and Americans within the last few days. There seems something almost incredible about this but then it is vouched for by a large number of miners and also a coroners inquest. This is the state of society that we have in this country; especially in the extreme north and south. Everybody carries a revolver by his side or a bowie knife and most of them both. If a person is irritable or flashy and gets insulted, the first

DANGEROUS CONSEQUENCES OF CARRYING DEADLY WEAPONS.

thing he does is to draw his revolver and either shoot the man through or knock him down. He doesn't stop to reason and let his better judgment dictate but gives way to the first impulse. Here we see the immorality and dangerous consequence of carrying deadly weapons. How would it look to you to go into the court house in Boston and, out of fifty men, see forty of them armed with pistols and knives? It would probably remind you of "days of Knight-errantry" instead of civilization and humanity. Judges in this country have had to shoot witnesses dead on the stand to save their own lives. This is truly a land of *chivalry* where *satisfaction* must be had. It was a curious sight to me to see two men go out in the street with nothing on but pants, shake hands in a friendly manner, and then fight just as long as they could move. Intemperance is the mother of all these crimes. You seldom see a strictly temperate man in trouble here. I think the greatest blessing that could be conferred upon this beautiful country would be to place a line of battle ships at the Golden Gate and sink every vessel bound in to Frisco with liquor aboard. Property should not be brought into account with the happiness and lives of a half million people.

AN UNACCEPTABLE JUDGEMENT.

By the way, the second morning when I was serving upon the *Grand Jury*, one man did not answer to his name. We reported him to the sheriff and he went in search of him and after an hour's hunt he found him, but so drunk that he couldn't walk without help. He tried to get him into the jury room, but he was perfectly hors de combat and immediately went to sleep. We let him lay there for awhile till the disgrace of some of the grand jurors being intoxicated presented itself to our minds and then we had him carried off. We then proceeded with our business till noon and appeared before His Honor to report.

The roll was called and all answered but this one. The foreman passed in the bills which we had found, whereupon the Judge enquired if we had been transacting business when one of the jurors was under the state of intoxication? The foreman told him "yes." The Judge then told us that these bills were not

JURY DUTY
IN STYLE.

valid and that the jurymen would have to be discharged and our work all done over again! We found about twenty bills and over two-thirds of them were from the immediate source of intemperance. But, enough of this. What I have written, grammatically, reads most horrid. This is partly because I have written so fast and partly because I am not capable of doing better.

Today, as you will observe, is the last of "54." It is now evening and I am seated in the old log cabin writing to "Little Fitz." I wonder what he is doing this eve? Probably interested in some poem or treatise. Poem, I think, for he's been very poetical of late. It is a wonder to me how he has learned so much and still so young! do people inherit talents or is their success attributable to perseverence and industry? Now, perhaps this question might admit of some discussion, but circumstances are unfavorable for that this evening, inasmuch as the rain is pouring down like fun. My soul is in arms and eager for the *Long Tom*. The boys have gone to bed whistling "Yankee Doodle" and I feel like singing anything but "Old Hundred." I went to the Post office today expecting the 5th of December mail would come in but it did not. Tuesday will probably bring it. We look forward to the arrival of the Atlantic mail with the same pleasure that little children do to Christmas or Thanksgiving. They are the bright spots in our monotonous existence. Last mail I wrote to Helen and Smith. This mail I think I shall write a line or two to Mary or Phoebe. That you may rise to five feet nine inches and a greater proportion mentally is the wish of Horace, who will not write more till the mail arrives. Adios.

SLUICING IN THE RAIN.

January 6th, 1855:

Well, Charlie, it is so late now in 1855 that I shall have to omit you a "Happy New Year," but hope your happiness will be none the less. Our new year commenced with a splendid rain, more acceptable to us than the wishes—formal—of a thousand passable friends. It rained all day Monday and Monday night, cleared off Tuesday morning, but again set in at night and rained incessantly till Thursday afternoon. Such a steady pour down, for forty hours, I never saw. It turned our creek into a small river, washed one of our reservoirs away, injured our ditches, filled up our pits with mud and water and, take it all around, did us a heap of damage. But we have all the trenches repaired now and shall commence operating in earnest Monday morning. We should have washed today but it was so cold last night that our hose froze completely solid and it was not till afternoon that we got the water through. We washed half of the day yesterday just for a commencer and obtained $40.50. We considered this the poorest dirt on the whole premises, but as "gold is where you find it," there is no telling with accuracy where the best is. In exposing myself to these rains, I have caught a very bad cold and, consequently, feel a little dull. Medication and a little carefulness will soon place me alright.

PATENT MEDICINE CURES
MADE YOU FEEL BETTER:
THEY WERE MOSTLY
ALCOHOL.

But, to something more interesting. Last Thursday, the 4th, the Great American Mail arrived of December 5th. I had the extreme pleasure of taking out of the Post Office for Mr. Spear and myself four letters and twelve papers. "O ecstasies of bliss too fierce to last forever!!" How a person can live in this country and be contented and not receive papers and letters from America, is more than I can conceive. I have found many and many a man who says he has not written home since leaving and many of them "49ers." But I am digressing. Your letter of November 30th, like all the rest, needs no praising. You have only to ask the Boys what I think of Little Fitz and his epistles to be satisfied of their acceptance. The only thing that "grated upon my nostrils" in your epistle was your mentioning "roast turkey, plum pudding, etc." for Thanksgiving. If you had known what a "Sensitive Mortal" I am in regard to such things, I think you would have omitted it! The 30th day of November I dined upon good sweet bread and fried ham. Do you suppose that made me drowsy? No sir! It only increased my appetite! O America! How often would I fly to thee and get a plum pudding and drink a glass of milk, but I cannot. You are a long way off!

By the way, I wish to ask you a few questions before I forget it. 1st. Does the Governor's Council of Massachusetts possess any Executive power? If, for instance, a case should come before the Council and the Governor's opinion be in the minority, which would prevail, or which be authentic? 2nd. How far will Telegraphic batteries, such as now in use, convey dispatches? Or how far, as a general thing, do they convey dispatches? And 3rd. I had another one but cannot possibly recall it, however, I will substitute this. Supposing I should return to America next summer and have $800 to appropriate to my good, now, in what manner could this be done most beneficial to myself? Taking it for granted that my school days are over. I have an impression as to the truth of the first two questions, but am not certain. The last one you can dispose of as you like. Perhaps, lay it on the *Table*.

I received a letter from John this mail, but betwixt you and I, I think he had better try again. I will answer all letters written me willingly, but when there is nothing to answer, I must beg to be excused. In my letters to Helen and Mary last mail this I tell them: that there is nothing in this world that will make me *delightfully happy* but a good cooking stove. Do you think I will get much sympathy?

As this mail does not leave for a few days, I may think of something more.

Your true friend, etc.
Horace C. Snow.

January 8th:

The mail yesterday, Charlie, brought me two more letters, one of which I am obliged to answer today. This deprives you of a few more lines, but perhaps no more news. I received a letter from my Cousin this mail stating that Mr. P. had been paid. He says he has written me twice or three times since then.

Horace.

LETTER 16

Miners In Waiting

Agua Frio, Cal.
February 6th, 1855

Dear Charlie:

Two weeks more have passed and with it all hopes of visiting America the coming summer. The moon has changed and brought no rain; the weather continues one beautiful, delightful, pleasant spell, not a cloud dots the sky, not a breath of air fans your brow, and not a sign is there for rain. Everything has the appearance of spring. The grass begins to look green, trees are budding, summer birds are returning, frogs have commenced peeping and we poor, rugged miners have commenced calculating—what is to become of us. If no rain should fall this spring, I shall be obliged to remain here another year. I suppose I could sell my interests here but could get nothing what they are worth. I was offered the other day $700 for about three-fourths of my thrown-up dirt, but nothing less than $1,000 would tempt me. My Brother asks $2,000 but this is rather high. However, it is acknowledged that when water comes we have the best show of any man on the creek; therefore, you can see that pecuniarily I have but little to think about. All that troubles me is how I am going to remain here another long year without seeing some of my old chums; without getting fresh papers every morning; without getting something good to eat; without enjoying some good society; and lastly, without seeing some pretty girls!! I have anticipated so much happiness in returning this summer that the idea of being disappointed is in no way agreeable. But I suppose it is all for the best, though we cannot realize it. There are a hundred men on this creek doing nothing now, half of them out of funds and considerable in debt. The most of these are Southerners who are too lazy to work an hour or two every day and pay their board, but loafing around waiting for a time when they can make money faster. This class have our heart-felt sympathy.— the *other way*. But we are going to take things as cool as we can. We are going to subscribe for ten or twelve papers pretty soon and have some news twice a month, though it be a little late. When I can get something fresh to read or as long as I can, I am very well contented but come to read the papers through twice, advertisements and all. I have a keen appetite for America. Your letter of December 30th and papers arrived the 3rd of this month and was a welcome New Year epistle. Charlie, though much I covet a letter from you every mail, yet I do not wish you, after working hard all day and particularly at writing, to sit up in the evening when you ought to be resting, to pen me a letter. I hope you do not feel under any obligation to answer all the letters I write you. Our circumstances are very different. I am busy outdoors all day and come evening it is an agreeable change for me to write, but you have to do the same thing that you were tired of at noon, when you long for some other recreation. Now, hereafter, unless you have plenty of time you will be perfectly justified in not writing me but once a month. Then I shall be your debtor should I write twice a month. I feel just as though I was the one that was benefitted and you only troubling yourself for acquaintance sake. Hereafter, take heed I shall write something every mail but can't promise it to be worth much. How I would like to be there enjoying those Mercantile Lectures with you. It must be a rare treat to listen to such men as Beecher, Benton and Houston, men who have the courage and independence to assert what they think to be right. If the Lectures are reported, I would like a copy very much.

Wednesday Eve. the 7th:
Since last night a very great change has taken place in the weather and present appearances indicate a storm. The wind is from the right direction and the clouds look watery but the

change has been so sudden that but little rain can be expected. However, if between this and next Monday we should have rain sufficient to go to washing and should continue to have till the 1st day of June, my anticipations may yet be realized. I have not deferred my hope yet and shall not as long as the atmosphere forebodes lucky times.

TRAVELING COSTUME
WORN BY THE WELL-
DRESSED MINER.

My Brother started last Monday for a short tour up North. I could but help thinking how different he looked to what a person would in New England starting on a similar journey. He went by horseback, as all travelling is done here. He wore spurs which were an inch in length, large leather leggings and a revolver. Self-protection is all that is thought of here.

Have I ever told you anything about our currency here? If not, I will say a few words which may be interesting. In the first place, it consists of just as many denominations as there are languages spoken. The majority of the Gold coin is American but nine-tenths of the silver is foreign. There are no cents and but very few half-dimes in the country. Therefore, the smallest piece of money made use of in making change is the dime. Till within a few months all pieces of money larger than a Mexican nine pence have passed for .25 cents, but so many one-franc pieces have been exported from France for speculation that the merchants have by a concerted movement cut them down to their original value—.18 cents. In purchasing goods, anything is sold by the bits worth—.12½ cents. One dime passes for a bit and four of them will buy just as much as a half dollar. In paying postage if there is due five cents and you hand them a quarter, you will get a dime in return. No one complains because no one stews for a bit. This is the case in the mines, though I hear at Frisco and the lower towns they are more exact. How curious it would seem to have a dozen coppers in my pocket to jingle. Change in some places in the mines is very scarce, but as all merchants buy gold dust and weigh as small sums as a bit, there is but little trouble. No news here in particular. There have been a good many murders in the country the past month, but they are so common that but little

THE PRINTING PRESS THAT CAME AROUND THE
HORN... A FOUR TO SIX MONTH TRIP.

notice is taken of them. I send you a Mariposa Chronicle, the only paper printed in this county. It resembles all the other mountain papers in the State. Being very uneasy concerning the weather, I must beg "extension" until next mail.

Yours truly,
Horace.

[100]

LETTER 17

Rain, Rain, Come Back Again

Agua Frio, California
February 23, 1855

Dear Charlie:

I had given up all hopes of receiving a letter from you this mail as several California mails have arrived since the Atlantic and did not go to the Post Office today fearing another disappointment, but, fortunately and happily and acceptably, a neighbor brought me this one letter and *four papers*. He also brought me word from the Postmaster that all mail matter for this mail must be in the office tomorrow afternoon. The first thing, of course, was to see what Little Fitz was up to, and then to peruse the papers.

And, by the way, "Industrious Nat" came in for a little attention before reaching the papers, as he found time, or took time, at the detriment of other business, to write me. Nat would make a splendid lawyer, if unintelligible chirography was the only criterion to judge by. I never shall get all the news from his letter until I have him read it himself.

News from the States seems to be very interesting this mail. Heavy failures, high prices of provisions, dull times, contagious diseases, political shenanigans, and infantile wedlocks—infantile in sense, if not in years—all come in for a share of public attention. How different are our wants in this great world. Take today, for instance; some wish credit, some beg extensions of payments, some wish food, some honor, some power, some love, and some more moderate than the rest only wish a good clear "Tom" stream of water. Yes, give some a good tom stream of water and all other things will be added. This is the case with me. From the 1st of last January to the 21st of February hardly a drop of rain fell on the banks of Agua Frio. It has been cloudy now for nearly a week, the wind blowing in all directions during the day and raining a very little during the nights. Up North the miners are lying idle because of the large quantities of snow, while down here it is too warm for comfort in the middle of the day.

24th, A.M.: No more rain this time, Charlie. This is just as beautiful a moon as ever was seen. West wind and not a cloud to be seen. Everybody now is looking forward to the next Full Moon. Old "forty-niners" bet high on rain then. Some put off the good time coming till the sun crosses the line, while others

VIGILANTE MOTTO: STRING THE RASCAL UP!

have given up expectations for rain and are preparing to realize them. I prophesy if we should have no more rain this winter that next summer or this year will exceed any other one in trouble and crime in California. The people have lost all confidence in the civil government and are taking the reins into their own hands. Woe be to the transgressor if the multitude once gets hold of him! The prosperity of the country is generally good. Large "strikes" are being made in different parts of the mines. Great excitement about the Kern River diggings, surging now and thousands of lazy loafers are winding their way there, not to mine, but to gamble and steal.

MINERS PURSUE EACH NEW STRIKE... FOLLOWED BY GAMBLERS, HONEST MERCHANTS AND DISHONEST CONFIDENCE MEN.

It is not the pioneer in this country that reaps the reward—the greater their success, the greater their dissipation. It is the sober second-thought individuals that profit by their new discoveries. Kern River is two hundred miles exactly south of here.

In regard to Mr. P., everything is all right. My Cousin has written me, though, I think I told you this before. I think you must be very busy and pretty hard-worked in the Traveller office. I couldn't stand—especially till I became used to it—this working evenings. This is the only part of the 24 hours that I can enjoy myself. Give me plenty to read and a room by myself or a cabin and I'm all right. If I should live here another year I think I should build me another cabin and live alone.

I did not send you a paper as I intended last mail, but send you two this. There is nothing particularly interesting in them more than that they come from California. Thank you for

those papers and hope to again next mail. Nothing new here.
Have been very busy lately prospecting. Must close for the *firm*
have been waiting for me for some time. Trouble you again
next mail.

Truly yours,
Horace.

MARIPOSA CHRONICLE:

WHITACRE & GOULD, EDITORS.

FRIDAY, FEBRUARY 3, 1854

COLORADO.—On account of the scarcity
of water the majority of miners are not
doing much in this camp; but there are
some few companies who are " puddling"
their dirt, and averaging from $10 to $20.
per day to the man.

MINING IN BEAR VALLEY.—We are informed by a gentleman living in Bear Valley, that the Mexicans and Chileans at
this place, are doing extremely well. In
a small gulch, lately struck, close to the
town, they have been averaging from $4
to $8 to the *battere.*

GUADALOUPE.—The mining intelligence
from this place, is encouraging. Those
working on the creek, are making good
wages; and one company, (J. Williams &
Co.,) working below Turner & Co.'s store,
are doing very well. The same company
have also a "surface claim," which avera-
ges from 2 to 25 cents to the pan. If there
was plenty of water in this section, there
are many more claims of the "same sort."

LETTER 18

Today We're Rich

Agua Frio, California
Friday Eve., March 9th, 1855

Dear Charlie:

Your poetic epistle of January 28th came to hand yesterday and has been read with a great deal of pleasure. I was so unprepared for such a production from you that two weeks will hardly allay the surprise. Therefore, I shall have to write this illiteral this mail and try next time to show my *Punkins* or *poetry*. However, you can't expect much from me as the muses never were known to enter an old Log Cabin—but once and that was the cabin of a young man who crossed the plains and wrote a poetical description home to his friends. I haven't the whole production, but remember a few passages, which I will quote for your benefit.

"In the year of '51,
I arrived in Mormondom,
And saw the Prophet, Brigham Young."

And so the production went on, growing more beautiful and sublime, till at last he made one desperate effort and concentrated his whole genius and fiery inspiration on the following lines:

"About the 21st of March,
I took up my line of march
and reached a place
of high renown called Hang Town."

Whether the author of this is alive now, I don't know, but my impression is that he is not, for who but Jupiter could stand such a Minerva from their hand.

Having the possible fate of this man before my eyes, I shall restrain myself sufficiently to survive the effort. Therefore, when you receive it you may allow that I am not Hors de Combat.

The good rains you speak of did not arrive here till the last day of February. The accounts you saw were probably of the first week in January. It is now nearly bedtime. All this very evening I have been cleaning and dividing our past week and a half's yield of gold. We commenced washing the 1st day of March and have washed every day and one night since— Sunday included! We have only had about thirty-six hours of rain but this has made glad the heart and yellow the pocket of many a miner. You may think it strange of my working on Sunday, but circumstances were such that I thought it justifiable. The rainy season is nearly passed and all the show we have to earn our food is when it rains or when there is water, and, as our chances are few for anything more than an occasional shower, we are obliged to improve them when they come or not at all. In these nine days we have taken out over $600.00 worth of gold and this is what I have had before me all evening. There was about $40 of the gold that was just as fine as fine sand and mixed with twice its weight of finer sand. This I had to separate and it was a very tiresome job, but the sight of such a *good pile*, and knowing that part of it was mine, made the task very easy. But unless it rains very soon again, I shall hardly handle as much gold for a long ten months. There is not now a "Tom" stream in the creek and did we not catch all that sand, we could do but little. I think with plenty of water for two months and our dirt paying about the same, that I could visit America the coming summer. There is a high wind tonight but it comes from a quarter which the "oldest inhabitants"—deer excluded—never saw rain, i.e. N.W.

However, I am contented and think of the good times coming. My brother has just informed me that all letters must be in the Post office tomorrow evening or not in season for this mail. How convenient it is to live where your letters and mail matter travel the distance of two hundred and fifty miles in the unprecedented time of six short days! and also to live where the mails never come regular or deposit regular. This letter

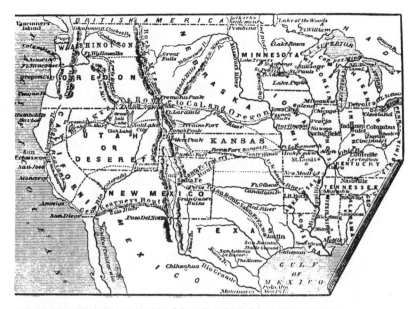

HORACE AND HIRAM SNOW COULD HAVE FOLLOWED THE
OVERLAND TRAILS TO CALIFORNIA, SEVERAL THOUSAND MILES OF
WILDERNESS, MOUNTAINS AND THE "GREAT AMERICAN DESERT," A
JOURNEY THAT LASTED MANY MONTHS...

THEY CHOSE THE SEA ROUTES.

1849. HIRAM SNOW SAILED
AROUND THE HORN, A VOYAGE
OF 17,000 MILES THAT TOOK FIVE
TO TWELVE MONTHS, DEPENDING
UPON THE SHIP, THE WEATHER
AND THE LUCK.
1854. HORACE SNOW CHOSE THE
SHORTER PANAMA ROUTE. HE
COVERED THE 5,382 MILES IN
ONLY FIVE WEEKS.

'BACK HOME,'
SO FAR AWAY
IN TIME AND
SPACE...WAS
'AMERICA' TO
HORACE AND
HIS FELLOW
GOLD-SEEK-
ERS.

arrangement is very pleasant, for you are always being continually taken by surprise. O America! America! What a paradise. But I must close and retire. I thought I should have had until Sunday to finish this in and write considerable more but the time is not allowed me. Not having worked very hard for sometime past till within a few days, I feel very tired and lame. We have been out before sunrise and never in till after sundown; therefore, I have retired very early every night. I am getting down on cooking when I work so hard. I must have a wife as soon as convenient. Select one for me! With your letter came the papers and Almanac. Many thanks for your kindness and trouble. Enclose a dollar as a present to you for the purpose of buying peanuts to eat while you have the "Blues." So appropriate! Shall do better the next time if the weather is favorable. If you answer this, pay me in the same coin.

Yours truly,
Horace.

LETTER 19

A Matter Of Health

Agua Frio, Cal.
April 10, 1855

Dear Charlie:

A few words of apology. Last mail you received no letter from me per agreement and have wondered why! After the 16th of March mail was ready—my own matter—I concluded that on the 18th of the same month, Sunday, I would commence that *poetical answer* and be in season for the 1st of April mail. But things were not to be so, or so it proved. On the 16th the fore finger of my right hand commenced swelling and on the 17th was very sore and quite painful. Poulticed it on the night of the 17th, day of the 18th, night of the 18th, and on the 19th began to grow better, 20th much better, and 21st commenced work very easily; therefore, during this affliction it was impossible for me to write. But you say I had plenty of time after this. So I did, but let's see. On the 22nd we had company all the evening, on the 23rd the same, 24th the same, and on the 25th exactly the same, and the 26th mail left Agua Frio. All these days I worked like a *white man* and was as tired as a dog at night. I shall try and not make any promises or if I do I shall try very hard to keep them. Shall not say when the poetical letter will come. We are now mining and have plenty of water. We had a powerful rain the 30th and 31st of March—being caused, so everybody says, by the full moon and the sun crossing the Equator, but our rains partake more of spring showers than storms and always clear off very warm. I have now given up all ideas of visiting America this summer. I shall have ample means to visit home and return again, but what will be the benefit? Unless I could remain at home with a small sum sufficient to start me in some kind of business, it is better for me to stay here. Had the mining season commenced two months earlier, as it ought to, I think my anticipations would have been realized—having been very moderate. To visit home this summer and return again, as I certainly shall—would place me nearly the same as one year ago. Therefore, in order to get satisfaction and accomplish what I would like to, I shall be obliged to remain here another year. This seems rather hard, just as you and I were going up to the White Mountains and away down on Cape Cod, but I suppose it is fair. I suppose if I should not return for several years that there would still be sand on the Cape and rocks around the White Mountains; therefore the interest will not entirely be gone. While traces of the original remain. When I do come, we will make up for lost time. But I will speak more of this some other time.

Your letters of February 18th and March 3rd, I have received, and still remain your debtor for them. Mr. Parker's sermon, Frank Leslie's New York Journal and all the papers mentioned have also arrived. For the abundant supplies of reading matter I am many more times thankful to you. Mr. Parker's is splendid. The more I read and hear of that man, the better I like him. Everything from him has a meaning, deep and easily understood. Such sermons as this and reports of those Lectures which you have sent me suit my tastes exactly. I have but just glanced over Houston's and Garrison's Lectures for the reason that my eyes have been very sore for the last ten days and are now. I have given up reading evenings at present and can only catch a few moments at meal time during the day. I was troubled just so with my eyes last spring. I think by taking good care of them they will soon be well.

You ask a few questions about how we manage our claims. First, do we own our claims? Yes. On this creek any American Citizen has the right to hold one claim for himself and one for each hired man! Miners, as a general thing, own their claims. I am connected with two companies. My Brother and I form one company and half of another. My Brother and I will probably work out all the ground we own this spring, but in the other company we claim six claims. The value of a claim is according to what it pays. We value our claims at $100 per claim. Though I think they are hardly worth it. I paid $100 for an interest in this ground last fall. We have already washed out four claims on this flat and have there six more claims. The ground upon which I am mining is within the boundaries claimed by Col Fremont. If Fremont gets his title confirmed—which rumor says he has—he will be a rich man—provided the miners will give the land up to him. If he attempts to hold the placer diggings, there will be serious trouble in this county.

THERE WILL BE SERIOUS TROUBLE AHEAD.

It is raining here most beautiful this evening. Our cabin is shingled with oak shingles and over this is a fly made of cotton drilling. Not a drop of water gets through. How splendid the rain sounds as it patters on the cloth. Would that you were here to talk over old Bridgewater and Model times. Two years ago now we were enjoying our first vacation. Would that my second one have been as short as the first! But, "It is an ill wind that blows nobody any good." Some good may come of it yet. Enclosed in this is a dollar's weight in fine gold and the same in black sand. I send them mixed but if you wish the gold separated, you first turn the gold and sand onto a newspaper and by blowing gently you will have them separated. I send you this so you may see all the different kinds of gold we have. My Brother intends now returning home this summer. He thinks considerable of going by way of China, but if he does not and goes directly home, I will send you a few more specimens. I commenced this sheet several days ago—intending, as I always say, to have written more but hard work and bad eyes and domestic affairs have limited it to this. Positively no failure next mail. There are many things that I wish to answer in your letters, but by and by, no, I will make no more promises. I must apologize again for using so much space for apologies. Whenever I receive such letters as this I think that the same space filled with news would be much more acceptable. You will please not notice or think of this. If it should rain tomorrow, I will try and write a little more.

Truly,

Horace.

MARIPOSA CHRONICLE:
FRIDAY, JANUARY 20, 1854.

THE FREMONT CLAIM.

As a matter of vital and paramount interest to the people of Mariposa as well as California at large, notwithstanding its great length, we publish entire the decision of Judge Hoffman of the U. S. District Court reversing the decree of the U. S. Land Commission he claim laid by Col. John Charles Fremont to the greater portion of Mariposa, and the richest portion of the Golden State.

The reason given for reversing the confirmation of the Land Commission must strike every one as being cogent and conclusive; "Confirmation strong as proofs of Holy writ."

A transcript of the record in this case, certified to the Supreme Court of the United States was sent on by the steamer of the 16th, and the early action of the highest judicial tribunal in the Union, settling this vexed question may be safely calculated upon. There is no doubt but that the able desision of Judge Hoffman in the premises will be affirmed by the Supreme Court, and that consequently what has been hitherto claimed as private property will be declared as belonging to the public domain.

Whatever "outside pressure" or side issues may be brought to bear upon the Land Commission (and we do not charge this is the case in the present instance) the ermine of the highest judicial Tribunal in the land cannot be soiled by filthy lucre.

JOHN C. FREMONT, AMERICAN EXPLORER-OF-THE-WEST, PURCHASED THE 44,000 ACRE SPANISH LAND GRANT, 'LAS MARIPOSAS' IN 1847. DISCOVERY OF GOLD BROUGHT MINERS INTO THE AREA. WHILE FREMONT WAS ATTEMPTING TO ESTABLISH HIS RIGHT TO THE LAND, GOLD-SEEKERS WERE STAKING CLAIMS AND WERE BUSILY REMOVING THE SURFACE GOLD. THE AGUA FRIO CLAIMS WORKED BY H. SNOW AND HIS PARTNERS WERE WITHIN 'LAS MARIPOSAS.' IF FREMONT PERFECTED HIS TITLE, HORACE AND HUNDREDS OF OTHER MINERS WOULD LOSE THEIR CLAIMS. IN 1859 THE COURTS CONFIRMED FREMONT'S RIGHT TO THE LAND AND THE MINERALS.

[112]

LETTER 20

Keeping Current By Subscription

Agua Frio, California
April 16th, 1855

Dear Charlie:

Once more, as usual, I appear before you to ask more favors. Had I any other friend in Massachusetts who would do these things without delay, I should not trouble you as much as I do now, but as they fail to answer letters, I think that they would be dilatory in performing business, therefore, the little confidence in them. If you should be actuated by the same principle in doing these favors for me that John is by teaching (the satisfaction of doing good to others), you will be amply paid, for all the inhabitants around Agua Frio will receive the benefits. Those papers, pamphlets, etc. which you have sent have visited five cabins just as regular as they have mine. With this principle of John's and the balance of remittance left, I hope, pecuniarily, you will be none the loser. The obligation I wish you to enter on account. The papers I wish you to subscribe for are the Boston Telegraph, Boston Journal, Boston Post, Waverly Magazine, Ballou's Pictorial, New York Tribune and one other, the selection of which I leave to you. I give you the choice of one partly to ascertain your taste and partly for fun. Any paper printed in the United States, whether religious, literary, political, or comical, no matter what, will be acceptable. You see, I have the three political parties represented, so as to be posted in them all and not yet prejudiced against either one, by sending all upon one side.

[113]

Yes, Charlie, the boys say that I must take another one and that one edited by a Lady. They say as I am going to keep an Old Bachelor's Hall that some restrictive influence will be needed over my habits and manners; therefore, you please select another one. Subscribe for the weeklies and have them directed to Horace C. Snow, Agua Frio, Mariposa County, California. Along with this is a twenty dollar piece to execute the favor. I was intending to send you five dollars more but the rascally Express Company ask $6.00 for freighting the $20 and so on. Therefore, the balance will be but little for your trouble. When my Brother returns he will call and see you and make the account straight.

Yours truly,
Horace C. Snow.

LETTER 21

Sudden Return
To 'America'

Boston
June 19, 1855

Dear Charlie:

As you have been informed, Snow has arrived in *America*. He intended to have written you before, but as these are the first lines that he has scribed to any person, you can consider yourself more honored—if it be an honor—than the rest of my acquaintances. I landed in New York the 6th day of June and from that time to this I haven't seen a moment's leisure time which I could spend in writing to anybody. I have not been home yet, but intend to go next Friday. How I came to return so suddenly, and thousands of other little things, I must omit till I see you, which I think will be before the 4th of July. I am going home and spend a week or ten days, then return to Boston and spend the 4th and then go back to Coos and help Father do his haying. Spear returned also. My Brother remains at Agua Frio. I am going out to Newton tomorrow and shall call at your Father's. Went to Bridgewater last Friday. Met Smith there, also Stephens and indefatiguable Nat. Spear accompanied us. Visited my sister yesterday at Bradford Seminary. Have not been out to Newton but twice, nor have not stayed there either night yet. Where I have been and what I have been doing since I returned I don't know, but one thing, I am half dead from so much visiting.

How and where you and I will spend our time together I shall leave altogether to you. In answer to this direct to

[115]

Whitefield, N.H. and tell me how you are situated. When I get home I shall have some time that I can spend in writing, but as long as I stay here I shall not have a moment's rest. Write to me as soon as you get this and we will soon understand each other. I shall be in Whitefield next Friday night certain. Excuse delay and brevity.

Yours truly,
Horace C. Snow.

"SNOW HAS ARRIVED IN AMERICA! HOW I CAME TO RETURN SUDDENLY . . . I MUST OMIT TILL I SEE YOU."

The 'Dear Charlie' letters leave us wondering! Why did Horace leave so suddenly? How did he get home? Did he take the 4,861 mile Nicaragua route? Or did he go by way of Panama, 5,382 miles from San Francisco to New York? And did he return home with a 'yellow pocket'?

HOMEWARD BOUND!

LETTER 22

Home, Sweet Home

Boston
October 25, 1855

Dear Charlie:

Good OLD Boston versus California! Where do you think I am today! Pacing the deck of some steamer on the Pacific or happily enjoying the comforts and society of friends in Boston? Aye, sir, here I is!!! Have not gone to California and am not going! I concluded not to go only two days before the Steamer sailed from New York. I went to New York first the same as though I was going and stayed ten days. Only a few persons knew what I was up to. My Cousin went on.

Those books I received in due season and was very thankful for them, but as I am not going, I consider the favor or presents hardly acceptable, because of a different use and will pay you well for them. I think them very interesting.

What I shall do now I hardly can tell. I am looking to get something to do in Boston. How long are you going to remain in New Hampshire? Think of settling there? Great excitement here owing to the Fair. City overrun with strangers. A boy is waiting to take this to the Post office. Will write you a letter after the fair is over and tell you why I did not go. Everything remains about the same. Stephens at Bridgewater, Spear in N.H., Miss H. in Boston, also Aunty of Whitefield. Remember me to your Uncle and Aunt, etc.

Yours truly,
Horace C.

ABOLITIONIST HORACE SNOW WAS IN THE
UNION ARMY DURING THE CIVIL WAR...

HE MARRIED
MARGARET
FOX BUTCHER

AND RETURNED TO CALIFORNIA TO TRY HIS HAND AT GOLD
MINING AGAIN FOR A VERY SHORT TIME.

IN HIS OCTOBER 7, 1854 LETTER TO CHARLIE, HORACE REMARKED
THAT HIS TASTES WERE "DECIDEDLY MERCANTILE." FOLLOWING
THIS INCLINATION, HE BECAME THE PROPRIETOR OF "SNOW & CO."
IN EUREKA. HE RAISED A FAMILY AND PURSUED A BUSINESS AND
AGRICULTURAL CAREER IN NORTHERN AND SOUTHERN CALI-
FORNIA.

H. C. SNOW.   H. K. SNOW.

SNOW & CO.,

Wholesale and Retail Dealers in

DRY GOODS, FANCY GOODS, CLOTHING,

BOOTS AND SHOES, HATS, CAPS, AND YANKEE NOTIONS.

EUREKA, HUMBOLDT CO., CAL.

IF THE "SNOW & CO." LETTERHEAD IS ANY INDICATION, IT WOULD
APPEAR THAT HORACE RETAINED THE SENSE OF HUMOR AND THE
YANKEE NOTIONS THAT MADE HIS LETTERS SO SPECIAL.